Journal of
Early
Childhood and
Infant
Psychology

Volume 6
2010

PACE UNIVERSITY PRESS   NEW YORK

ISSN 1554-6144
ISBN 978-1-935625-04-9

Address Subscription Inquiries to:

Pace University Press
41 Park Row, Room 1510
New York, NY 10038

www.pace.edu/press
(212) 346-1405

Journal of Early Childhood and Infant Psychology

Editor
Anastasia E. Yasik
Pace University—New York City

Associate Editors
Barbara A. Mowder
Pace University—New York City
Florence Rubinson
Brooklyn College of the City University of New York

Editorial Review Board

Phyllis Ackman
Pace University—New York City

Vincent C. Alfonso
Fordham University

Stephen J. Bagnato
University of Pittsburgh

Anni Bergman
New York University

Zeynep Biringen
Colorado State University

Bruce Bracken
College of William & Mary

Susan Chinitz
Albert Einstein College of Medicine

Gerard Costa
Youth Consultation Service Institute for Infant & Preschool Mental Health

Grace Elizalde-Utnick
Brooklyn College of the City University of New York

Nancy Evangelista
Alfred University

Madeline Fernández
Pace University—New York City

Gilbert M. Foley
Yeshiva University

Paul C. McCabe
Brooklyn College of the City University of New York

David McIntosh
Ball State University

Gail Ross
New York Presbyterian Hospital

K. Mark Sossin
Pace University - New York City

Mark D. Terjesen
St. John's University

Susan Vig
Children's Evaluation and Rehabilitation Center

Serena Wieder
Silver Spring, Md.

Editorial Assistant
Christine Pearston

Editorial Policy: The Journal of Early Childhood and Infant Psychology (JECIP) is a publication of the Association of Early Childhood and Infant Psychologists (AECIP). One aspect of AECIP's mission is to provide a vehicle for networking within early childhood and infant psychology, including fostering research, scholarship, and professional interactions. This journal (JECIP) focuses on publishing original contributions from a broad range of psychological perspectives relevant to infants, young children (up to age 8), parents, and caregivers. Manuscripts incorporating evidence-based research, theory and applications within clinical, community, developmental, neurological, and school psychology perspectives are considered. In addition to data-based research, the journal accepts test and book reviews, position statements, literature reviews, program descriptions and evaluations, clinical studies, and other professional materials of interest to psychologists working with infants, young children, parents, families, and caregivers. Proposals for mini-series may be made to the Editor.

Format: Manuscripts should be original work not currently submitted for publication to other journals. Authors must follow the guidelines of the *Publication Manual of the American Psychological Association (Sixth Edition)*. Manuscripts may not exceed 35 double-spaced pages in length, including the cover page, abstract, references, tables and figures.

Submission: Submit an electronic copy of the manuscript for editorial review. Avoid including any identifying author information in the text. Selection of manuscripts is based on blind peer review. Include a cover page with the following information: the title of article, author(s) full name(s), title(s), institution or professional affiliations, and mailing and email address of primary author. The cover page will not be sent to reviewers.

Selection Criteria:
- Importance of topic in early childhood and infant psychology
- Theory and research related to content
- Contribution to professional practice in early childhood and infant psychology
- Clear and concise writing

Submit manuscripts to the Editor at the following address:
Anastasia E. Yasik
Editor, JECIP
Psychology Department, Pace University
41 Park Row
New York, New York 10038
(212) 346-1801
Email: jecip@pace.edu

Journal of Early Childhood and Infant Psychology

Volume 6, 2010

Helping Our Toddlers, Developing Our Children's Skills (HOT DOCS):
A Parenting Intervention to Prevent and Address Challenging Behavior in Young Children

Jillian L. Williams, Kathleen H. Armstrong,
Heather Agazzi, & Kathy L. Bradley-Klug
University of South Florida

This study evaluated a behavioral parent training curriculum designed to teach caregivers a problem-solving approach to understand and address their children's challenging behaviors. Participants included 399 caregivers of children between the ages of 18 months to 6 years, 11 months. Participants' knowledge, attitudes, and perceptions of their children's behavior were evaluated using a pre/post knowledge test, rating scales of child problem behavior, and weekly progress monitoring forms for caregiver behavior at home. Upon completion of the parent training program, significant increases in caregiver knowledge and significant decreases in caregivers' perceptions of the severity of child problem behaviors were demonstrated. Participants reported high levels of satisfaction with the program on an evaluation survey. Findings support the potential effectiveness of this parent training program to address the challenging behaviors of young children.

After nearly three decades of cross-disciplinary research, professionals in the fields of psychology, education, and medicine are no longer surprised that their client lists, student rosters, and appointment schedules are filled with young children displaying challenging behaviors. The most commonly cited challenging behaviors in young children (between the ages of 2 and 7 years old) include sleeping difficulties, mealtime and feeding issues, toilet training, temper tantrums, aggression, sibling rivalry, and noncompliance. Recent research has shown that approximately 15-25% of all typically developing preschool children have chronic levels of behavior problems that fall within the mild to moderate range (Campbell, 1995; Keenan & Wakschlag, 2000; Knapp, Ammen, Arstein-

All correspondence should be addressed to Jillian Williams, Ph.D, University of South Florida, Division of Child Development, Department of Pediatrics, 13101 N. Bruce B. Downs Blvd., Tampa, FL 33612. Electronic mail may be sent to: jwillia6@health.usf.edu.

Kerslake, Poulson, & Mastergeorge, 2007; Lavigne et al., 1996). Even greater are prevalence rates of chronic behavior problems for minority children and/or children in low-income families, with estimates reaching up to 35% (Gross et al., 2003; Webster-Stratton, 1998).

The long-term outcomes associated with early-onset challenging behavior in young children have been well-documented (Coie & Dodge, 1998; Dishion, French, & Patterson, 1995; Kazdin, 1995; Reid, 1993; Tremblay 2000). In general, the earlier the problem behavior develops the more stable and intense the associated negative outcomes are over time. Dishion and colleagues found that early-appearing behavior problems in a child's preschool career are the single best predictor of delinquency in adolescence, gang membership, and adult incarceration. Other researchers have identified similarly poor long-term outcomes related to academic and school performance. Kazdin (1993) and Tremblay (2000) concluded from their research that preschoolers with challenging behaviors are at a greater risk of experiencing school failure than typically developing children.

In response to research demonstrating the rapid and enduring increase in the prevalence rates of young children with challenging behavior and the associated negative long-term outcomes, professionals across disciplines have developed a variety of interventions to help prevent and treat these behaviors. Behavioral parent training delivered in a group format is one such intervention, which has been shown to be both an effective and economical treatment to empower parents to prevent and address challenging behavior in young children (Lundahl, Risser, & Lovejoy, 2006; Maughan, Christiansen, Jenson, Olympia, & Clark, 2005; Nelson, 1995; Sandall & Ostrosky, 1999; Smith & Fox, 2003).

Despite the available evidence supporting the effectiveness of early intervention, there is a lack of services, resources, and empirically-supported interventions available to caregivers of young children displaying challenging behavior (Kazdin & Kendall, 1998; Knitzer, 2007; Walker et al., 1998). Based on the abundance of research supporting the primary role of parents and caregivers in young children's emotional and behavioral development, it follows that the most logical target for prevention and early intervention efforts would be improving caregiving skills and enhancing the caregiver-child relationship (Knitzer). Thus, group-based parent training would be an economical and ecologically-based system for providing children and families with the knowledge, skills, and support they need to prevent and correct challenging behaviors (Smagner & Sullivan, 2005). The ability of one child care professional to simultaneously meet the needs of multiple families and children at once dramatically increases the efficiency of limited resources, professionals, and funding sources.

Historically, one of the major theories guiding the inquiry into chronic behavior problems in young children was Skinner's (1953) theory of behaviorism. At its foundation, behaviorism postulates that all behavior is observable and functional. Behaviorism relies on the manipulation of antecedents and consequences and the effects of reinforcement and punishment as a means of changing and shaping behavior. In addition to approaching the study of challenging behavior in young children from a behavioral theoretical framework, it is necessary to view the problem through an ecological model of child development (Bronfenbrenner, 1979). An ecological model takes into account biological, sociological, and psychological domains of child development and functioning (Sontag, 1996). From an ecological perspective, manipulation of a child's environment, including the behavior of caretakers, will directly impact the child's behavior (Bronfenbrenner). Given the above, an intervention program designed with principles from behavioral and ecological models in mind would seem promising.

Helping Our Toddlers, Developing Our Children's Skills (HOT DOCS; Armstrong, Lilly, & Curtiss, 2006) is a behavioral parent training program, which incorporates both behavioral and ecological perspectives in its theoretical framework. HOT DOCS meets the following criteria for a behavioral intervention: a) centers around an operant model of behavior, b) provides caregivers with detailed information on effective caregiving strategies, c) focuses on control of antecedents instead of punitive consequences, and d) enhances generalization from the training setting to the home setting. HOT DOCS was designed to teach parents a problem-solving process based upon the foundation of behavioral principles (e.g., antecedents, consequences, and function of behavior) delivered in parent-friendly language. Unlike other parent training programs that focus on teaching parents to fix specific behavior problems, HOT DOCS teaches caregivers to use a step-by-step method to identify features of the environment and interpersonal interactions that may contribute to the reinforcement or maintenance of current and future problem behaviors. HOT DOCS also focuses on instructing caregivers to recognize that children may use challenging behaviors because they lack the knowledge or skills to use more appropriate behaviors. Program developers note that HOT DOCS is different from other existing parent training programs because it directs caregivers to teach children new or replacement skills instead of focusing on contingency management strategies designed to eliminate problem behaviors (Armstrong & Hornbeck, 2005).

HOT DOCS also is unique in that the same curriculum can be delivered to parents, relatives, other caregivers, and child service professionals all in the same group at the same time. This allows parents to bring their support network with them to classes, enhancing the consistency of skill implementation across caregivers and across settings outside of the training session. Other programs such as Incredible Years (Webster-Stratton, 1998) and Triple P-Positive Parenting Practices (Sanders, 1999) have separate curricula for parents, children, teachers, and caregivers.

Another major difference between HOT DOCS and existing parent training programs is the total time required for curriculum delivery. The HOT DOCS program is delivered over six consecutive weekly sessions of 2 hours each for a total of 12 hours of classroom-based instruction. Other programs average 12-30 weekly sessions or a total of 24-60 hours of training. The HOT DOCS program is in its fourth year of implementation, but no comprehensive study of the impact of the intervention on caregivers' knowledge and perceptions of target children's behavior has been undertaken.

The purpose of the current study was to serve as an evaluation of participants' knowledge and attitudes and as an investigation of participants' perceptions of target children's behavior following participation in the HOT DOCS parent training program by answering the following research questions:

1. What is the impact on caregiver knowledge of child development, behavioral principles, and parenting strategies as a result of participation in the HOT DOCS parent training program?

2. Do caregivers perceive their child as having more problem behavior than a normative sample prior to participation in the HOT DOCS program?

3. To what extent do caregivers perceive a decrease in child problem behavior following their participation in the HOT DOCS program?

4. What is the frequency and ease of use of the weekly parenting tips as reported by caregivers?

5. What are caregivers' overall perceptions of the HOT DOCS parent training program?

Overview of the HOT DOCS Parent Training Program

The HOT DOCS parent training program is delivered in 6 sessions, the objectives of which intend to teach specific behavioral strategies. Each of the sessions lasts approximately 2 hours and follows a prescribed routine, including 30 minutes of socialization and peer support during a light dinner, review of previously taught material and weekly skill use, and 1 hour of new instruction. Incorporated within each session are lecture, practice exercises, group problem solving activities, role play, and video vignettes. Refer to Table 1 for a summary of instructional topics for each HOT DOCS session. As a formal evaluation of the program is being completed, the first session also includes a discussion of the research consent procedures, collection of demographic information, a knowledge pretest, and a pre-test behavior rating scale. The sixth session concludes with participants completing a post-test and satisfaction survey. Participants complete the post-test behavior rating scales by mail, 2 months after the final session.

To reinforce learning objectives, a Parenting Tip and a Special Play Activity are included as homework for each session. Parenting Tips are specific skills participants may use to prevent and address challenging behavior and are linked to each session's content. For example, in session 2 participants are taught about the important role that predictable and consistent routines play in the healthy development of a child and how routines affect behavior in young children. As such, parents are asked to evaluate their daily routines with their children and identify the parts that are going well and those in need of some modification. The session's tip is to 'catch them being good' during the natural routines to teach caregivers the importance of praising their children for behaviors that are appropriate. The sessions' content build on one another starting with the very basics of child development, moving to routines and development, then the basics of behavior analysis are introduced, followed by an overview of preventions and interventions to support positive behavior and manage challenging behaviors in young children. The program concludes with a review of content and a brief presentation on caregiver stress levels, how to recognize stress, and appropriate actions to take when the stress is impacting caregiver functioning.

To document use of these tips, HOT DOCS Tip Tracker sheets help participants to keep a record of the number of days they use the skill, rate how difficult or easy the skill is to use each day, and provide specific examples of how they use the skill with their children each week. Special Play Activities are developmentally-based play activities to promote parent-child interactions and provide teachable moments for practicing and reinforcing children's new skills. Participants are provided with inexpensive toys to engage their child in the play activity and are given explicit instructions on how to use special play activities in ways that promote development of motor, communication, and social-emotional skills.

All of the HOT DOCS materials, presentations, and handouts are available in English and Spanish. The Spanish adaptation was developed and field tested by a team of bilingual students and staff from a university in the southeastern U.S., including a fellow in internal medicine and pediatrics who was originally from Ecuador; a master of public health graduate student with a medical degree, who

Table 1

Topic, Parenting Tip, and Special Play Activity for Each HOT DOCS Session

Session	Topic	Parenting tip	Special play activity
1	Early childhood development	Use positive words	Bubbles
2	Routines and rituals	Catch them being good	Reading
3	Behavior and development	Use a calm voice	Coloring
4	Preventing problem behavior	Use preventions	Fun dough
5	Teaching new skills	Follow-through	Balls
6	Managing parent stress	Take time for yourself	Free choice

Note. n = 260

was originally from Nicaragua; a doctoral intern in school psychology, who spoke Spanish as a second language; and a parent and HOT DOCS graduate, who was originally from Colombia (Agazzi et al., 2010).

Method

Participants

In the first session, trainers explained to participants that research was being conducted on the HOT DOCS program and they were asked to complete a consent form if they were willing to allow their data to be included in the research. If participants declined the opportunity to participate in the research study, they completed the training and required documents but their data were not included in any subsequent analyses. Individuals who consented to participation in the research study were assigned a unique identification code so that all data would remain confidential. It was made clear that participants could change their minds and revoke consent at any time during participation in the program.

Participants included parents, caregivers (i.e., biological relatives, foster parents, and legal guardians), and other professionals (e.g., speech therapists, early interventionists, daycare workers) whose children or clients displayed challenging behaviors. Participants were recruited through community advertisement or referred by health care providers. A total of 399 participants attended three or more (at least 50%) of the sessions in one of 43 classes conducted between April 2006 and May 2008 (30 delivered in English and 13 delivered in Spanish), data from which are described in this paper.

Participants were 71.8% female ($n = 296$), ranged in age from 19 to 69 years ($M = 34.3$, $SD = 8.17$), and reported their race or ethnicity as Caucasian (47.9%), Hispanic or Latino (37.7%), African American (8.6%), Other (3.2%), Asian (1.9%) or Native American (0.6%). Participants' reported levels of education varied from less than a high school diploma to a graduate level degree, with the largest percentage of participants (28.2%) reporting that they received a degree from a 4-year college ($n = 110$). Of the female participants, 242 reported being the child's mother or adoptive/foster mother, 40 were child service providers, 11 were the child's grandmother, and 3 were another female relative (e.g., aunt, sister). Of the male participants, 99 reported being the child's father or adoptive/foster father and 4 reported being the child's grandfather.

Target children.   Children ranged in age from 18 months to 6 years, 11 months old ($M = 41.3$ months or 3.4 years old, $SD = 21.7$ months). Of the children in the sample with preexisting diagnoses as indicated by parent report, 37 (10.2%) were children with a diagnosis on the autism spectrum including Pervasive Developmental Disorder (ASD/PDD), 28 (7.2%) were children with various medical or genetic conditions (e.g., hearing/vision impairments, epilepsy, Down syndrome, failure to thrive), 11 (2.6%) were children with developmental delays,

10 (2.6%) were children with speech or language impairments, 4 (1.0%) were children with behavior disorders, 3 (0.6%) were children with Attention-Deficit/Hyperactivity Disorder (ADHD), and 39 (10.2%) were children with multiple delays or disorders.

Measures

HOT DOCS Demographics Form. *The Demographics Form* was developed by the HOT DOCS authors in order to collect standardized information about the participants and children. This form includes 10 questions including participants' gender, age, target child's age, age(s) of other children in the home, type and name of health insurance, participants' relationship to targeted child, ethnicity, and level of education.

HOT DOCS Knowledge Test. The *Knowledge Test* was also developed by the HOT DOCS authors in order to assess participants' knowledge of child development, behavioral principles, and parenting strategies prior to and subsequent to participation in HOT DOCS classes. The test consists of 20 "True/False" statements and takes approximately 10 minutes to complete. Although the test includes items from various areas of knowledge covered in the parenting program, there are not enough items per area to investigate cluster scores. No information on reliability or validity was available for this instrument. For the purposes of this study, only total scores were recorded and analyzed. Total scores were computed by coding each correct response as a "1" and each incorrect response as a "0" and summing the total points for each participant.

HOT DOCS Tip Tracker Sheets. The *Tip Tracker* sheets were developed by the HOT DOCS authors to monitor, on a daily basis, caregivers' use of the Parenting Tips as practiced at home. Participants used a 5-point Likert-type scale to rate the ease of use of the specific parenting skill of the week with their child. The Likert scale ranges from 1 = *Very difficult* to 4 = *Easy*. In addition, a response option *Did not use skill* is provided. Participants were asked to circle this option if they did not use the skill that day. The sheet also provides space for participants to give specific examples of how they used the parenting tip with the target child.

Behavior Rating Scales. The *Child Behavior Checklist* (CBCL; Achenbach, 2001) was selected to assess participants' perceptions of the severity of children's problem behaviors. The CBCL is a psychometrically sound instrument, as evidenced by validity and reliability estimates (Achenbach). CBCL rating scales were completed at the first session and again 6 to 8 weeks post-training at the booster session.

HOT DOCS Program Evaluation Survey. The *Program Evaluation Survey* was developed by the HOT DOCS authors to assess participants' perceptions of the effectiveness of the parent training program. The survey consists of eight statements about the benefits of HOT DOCS to participants, the teaching skills of HOT DOCS trainers, and the impact of the program on child and family behaviors and relationships. Participants were asked to respond on a 4-point Likert-type scale as "Strongly Agree," "Agree," "Disagree," or "Strongly Disagree." The survey also consists of five questions with response options provided, which prompted participants to share their perceptions on the usefulness of the program as well as any suggestions for future trainings or improvements to the current program.

Procedures

Demographic information, knowledge-based pre- and post-tests, structured behavior rating scales, weekly progress monitoring forms, and social validity and acceptability measures were collected. The Demographics Form and the Knowledge Pretest were completed by participants during the first session. Behavior rating scales were completed on each child and returned by the second session. Individual Tip Tracker sheets were completed by participants each session to document ease of skill implementation over the week. Tip Tracker sheets were completed for each of the first through the fifth sessions. Participants completed the Knowledge Posttest during the final session of training. Two months after the final session a post-test behavior rating scale was administered. During the 2 years in which data were collected no significant modifications were made to the HOT DOCS curriculum or data collection procedures.

Results

Research Question 1: Participant Knowledge

What is the impact on caregiver knowledge of child development, behavioral principles, and parenting strategies as a result of participation in the HOT DOCS parent training program?

A dependent means t-test was calculated between participants' pre-test and post-test scores on the HOT DOCS Knowledge Test. Only 277 out of 399 participants who completed the HOT DOCS Demographic Form also completed both the pre- and post-Knowledge Test, attended three or more sessions, and signed the IRB consent form. The results of the t-test indicate that the participants' mean post-test score ($M = 17.30$, $SD = 1.79$) was significantly higher than the participants' mean pre-test score ($M = 15.95$, $SD = 2.09$), $t(276) = 11.20$, $p < .001$. The effect size was large ($d = 1.13$).

Research Question 2: Participants' Perceptions of Severity of Problem Behavior

Do caregivers perceive their child as having more problem behavior than a normative sample prior to participation in the HOT DOCS program?

Descriptive statistics were used to analyze the severity levels of participants' perceptions of child problem behavior prior to participating in the parent training program. A chi-square goodness of fit analysis was calculated ($\alpha = .01$) using the observed number of scores in the sample in the Non-Significant (T-scores less than 65), Borderline (T-scores between 65 and 69), and Clinically Significant (T-scores greater than or equal to 70) categories on the Internalizing and Externalizing scales of the CBCL and the expected number of scores in each of the three descriptive categories as predicted for a normal distribution of scores in a national sample. According to the CBCL manual, a normal distribution of scores predicts that for any given sample of children 93.94% of ratings will fall within the Non-Significant category, 3.79% will fall within the Borderline category, and 2.27% of ratings will fall within the Clinically Significant category (Achenbach, 2001). The ratings of participants in this sample were compared to normative information from a national sample in order to investigate the degree to which the participants in HOT DOCS were representative of the larger population. As expected, participants in the sample indicated greater levels of problem behavior than the general population.

For the Internalizing subscale, the test was statistically significant, X^2 (1, $N = 265$) = 992.51, $p < .001$, suggesting a significant difference between the expected frequency and observed frequency of scores in each descriptive category of the Internalizing subscale. Based on participants' perceptions, 13 times the number of children expected to have scores in the Clinically Significant range were found in this sample. The effect size for scores on the Internalizing subscale was large ($w = 1.508$). Similar results were found for the Externalizing subscale where a significant difference between the expected frequency and observed frequency

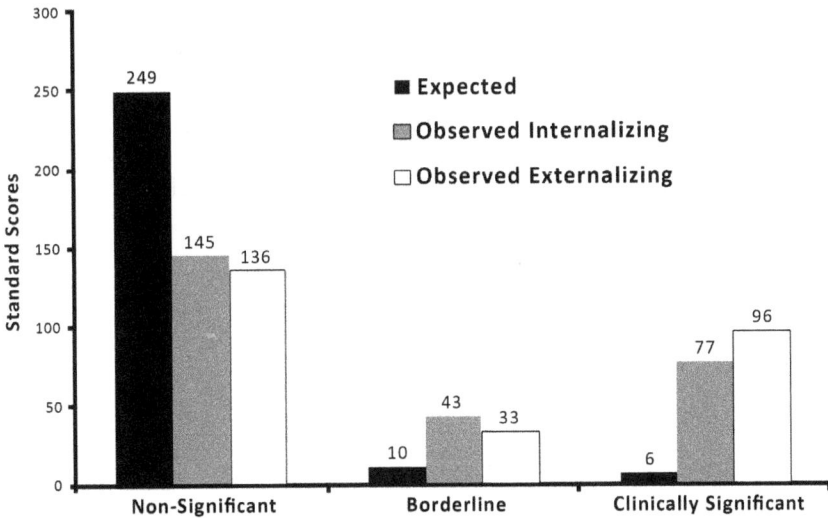

Figure 1. Number of expected and observed CBCL T-scores by descriptive category.
Note. n = 265; Non-Significant = T-scores less than 65; Borderline = T-scores between 65 and 69; Clinically Significant = T-scores greater than 70.

of scores in each descriptive category was observed, $X^2(1, N = 265) = 1454.18$, $p < .001$. The observed number of children in the sample whose Externalizing subscale scores fell within the Clinically Significant range was nearly 16 times the number expected to fall within that range and the effect size was large ($w = 1.823$) suggesting statistical and clinical significance. A graphic comparison of observed and expected frequencies of scores for the Internalizing and Externalizing scales is shown in Figure 1.

Research Question 3: Changes in Perceptions of Problem Behavior

To what extent do caregivers perceive a decrease in child problem behavior following their participation in the HOT DOCS program?

A two-factor repeated measures analysis of variance (ANOVA) was conducted to analyze the differences between participants' pre- and post-test scores on the Internalizing and Externalizing scales of the CBCL. The two within-subjects (repeated) factors were type of scale (A) (i.e., Internalizing and Externalizing) and time (T) (i.e., pre-test and post-test). Seventy-eight participants completed and returned both pre- and post-test CBCL rating scales. Means and standard deviations of pre- and post-test rating scale scores on the two subscales of the CBCL are reported in Table 2.

Results revealed a non-significant interaction effect ($p > .05$), a statistically significant main effect for time, $F(1, 77) = 12.30, p < .01$, and a significant main effect for scale, $F(1, 77) = 10.00, p < .01$. The main effect for Time (T) was followed up with a comparison of CBCL pre-test and post-test overall mean scores (i.e., marginal means) and results indicated that participants' perceived severity of children's problem behavior was greater at pre-test ($M = 58.93$) as compared to post-test ($M = 55.22$) across both the Internalizing and Externalizing scales. On the CBCL, higher scores indicate more severe levels of problem behavior; therefore, a decrease in scores from pre-test to post-test indicates participants' perceived children to have less severe levels of problem behavior following

Table 2

Means and Standard Deviations of Pre- and Posttest CBCL Scores by Scale

CBCL Scales	Pretest		Posttest		Marginal Means
	M	*SD*	*M*	*SD*	
Internalizing	57.05	10.09	53.99	11.64	55.52
Externalizing	60.81	12.51	56.44	12.04	58.93

Note. n = 78

participation in the program. Follow-up of the main effect for scale (A) was done by examining the overall CBCL Internalizing and Externalizing mean scores across time (i.e., Internalizing pre-test + post-test mean; Externalizing pre-test + post-test mean). The mean Internalizing scale score ($M = 55.52$) was significantly lower than the mean Externalizing scale score ($M = 58.93$). This finding indicates that participants' perceived severity of children's externalizing problem behavior (e.g., aggression, non-compliance) was greater than the perceived severity of children's internalizing problem behavior (e.g., depression, anxiety, withdrawal).

Research Question 4: Weekly Progress Monitoring

What is the frequency and ease of use of the weekly parenting tips as reported by caregivers?

The frequency of use per week of each parenting skill was computed from the weekly Tip Tracker forms. An average of 58% of participants returned completed Tip Tracker forms each of the five weeks that homework was assigned. Each week's data were analyzed separately as a different skill is assigned each week. Mean daily ratings were computed across participants and across skills for each day of the week in which the skill was assigned. Mean daily ratings were derived by averaging the ratings of ease or difficulty of use (1 = more difficult, 4 = easier) reported by participants in the 7 days immediately following the class which provided instruction in the use of the Parenting Tip. In the case that a participant reported not using the skill one or more of the days during the week it was assigned, the average for that participant's ratings was calculated based on the number of days the participant did use the skill.

A visual analysis of the graph displaying average daily ratings of ease or difficulty of use (see Figure 2) indicated differential participant ratings of ease of use across the five skills. Participants rated *Catch Them Being Good* ($M = 3.37$), as being the easiest skill to implement at home, followed by *Use Preventions* ($M = 3.04$), *Use Calm Voice* ($M = 3.03$), *Follow Through* ($M = 2.98$), and *Use Positive Words* ($M = 2.82$). Overall, all five skills followed a similar pattern of ease or difficulty of use based on visual analysis. Specifically, over the course of the week participants' ratings of ease of use slightly improved.

Research Question 5: Social Validity and Acceptability

What are caregivers' overall perceptions of the HOT DOCS parent training program?

Participants' mean ratings of satisfaction with the HOT DOCS program were computed using quantitative data obtained from the HOT DOCS Program Evaluation Survey. A total of 272 participants completed the Program Evaluation Survey. The majority of participants agreed that the *HOT DOCS* program met their expectations (100% Strongly Agree, 0% Agree), that the trainers were

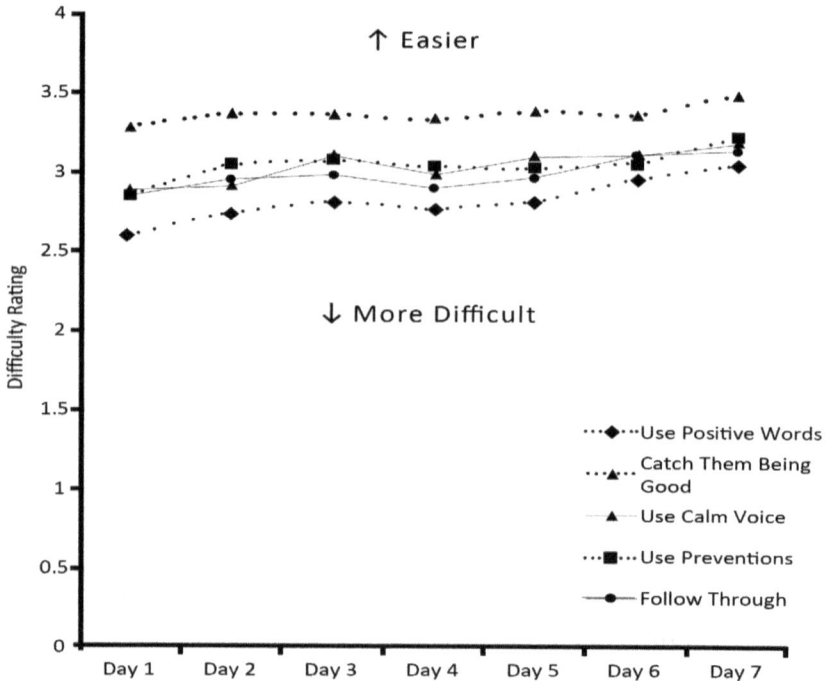

Figure 2. Average daily parent ratings of ease or difficulty of skill use at home.
Note: Average n = 234

knowledgeable and effective instructors (72% Strongly Agree, 26% Agree), that the Parenting Tips were beneficial (71% Strongly Agree, 26% Agree), and that the program positively impacted parenting attitudes and practices (72% Strongly Agree, 26% Agree). The statements for which some participants (<3%) marked *Disagree* or *Strongly Disagree,* all related to the participants' ability to implement parenting strategies presented in class, changes in children's behavior at home, and the participants' overall evaluation of the program. These data indicate that for a few participants, this level of intervention was not matched appropriately to the level of severity of problem behavior the child demonstrated in the home.

Participants' perceptions of the usefulness of information learned in HOT DOCS, their opinions on the value of the program, and suggestions for future trainings also were computed. The response options for all items on the survey were derived from a thematic analysis of free responses to the same questions provided by participants in a pilot study conducted with previous HOT DOCS cohorts.

Question #1 on the survey (*n* = 262) asked participants, "How are you using the information you learned in *HOT DOCS?*" and provided five options for participants to endorse. Participants were directed to check all boxes that applied. Response choices for Question #1 included use of a specific skill, improved relationship with child/others, sharing information with others, change in parenting attitude, and problem-solving behaviors. The majority of participants (87%) endorsed the response option, "using a specific skill." Participants' verbatim comments included "we have used calm voice and positive words and it does work," "to teach them how to do routines and rituals," "we mostly use prevention techniques," and "implemented a timer at bed time and gave warnings."

To respond to question #2 on the survey, "Have you shared information from HOT DOCS with...?" participants were instructed to check the boxes of all the people with whom they had shared information. A majority of the 272 participants reported sharing information from the program with friends (73%), a spouse or partner (70%), and other family members or relatives (69%). A smaller percentage of participants reported sharing information with an interventionist, therapist, or teacher (35%), other acquaintances (11%), or a pediatrician (9%). Two participants (7%) indicated that they had not shared information with anyone.

Question #3 on the survey ($n = 229$), asked participants, "What suggestions do you have for future HOT DOCS trainings?" As shown in Table 3, nearly 34% of participants ($n = 77$) indicated that the program would benefit from increasing

Table 3

Caregivers' Recommendations to Improve HOT DOCS

Response Options	n	%
More time for instruction	77	33.6
Nothing, fine as is	74	32.3
Changes to scheduling or location	44	19.2
Specify training by child's age or disability	9	3.93
Involve children and families	8	3.49
Train other professionals	8	3.49
More movies, examples, and scenarios	5	2.18
Provide additional resources	3	1.31
Changes to food	2	0.09
More relaxation training	2	0.09

Note. n = 229

Table 4

HOT DOCS Program Components Valued by Caregivers

Response options	n	%
Aquiring specific skills	203	78.1
Support and interaction with other caregivers	126	48.5
Problem-solving skills	126	48.5
Provision of materials	116	44.6
Instructors' knowledge and support	20	7.70
Validation of current parenting skills and abilities	8	3.08
Homework weekly review	5	1.92

Note. n = 260

the time for training and instruction while 32% of participants ($n = 74$) responded that no improvements should be made to HOT DOCS.

Question #4 on the survey ($n = 260$), asked "What did you value most?" and respondents were instructed to check all that applied. As shown in Table 4, the majority of the participants (78%, $n = 203$) who responded to this item indicated that they valued specific skills they acquired the most. Verbatim responses within this theme included: "teaching about calmness and timers," "activities each week," "teach my son positive words," "I learned new techniques that really worked," and "the preventions that I can put in place to hopefully avoid melt downs and behavior problems."

Summary

Results of this study revealed a significant and meaningful increase in caregivers' knowledge of child development, behavioral principles, and parenting strategies following their participation in HOT DOCS. Prior to beginning HOT DOCS, a significantly greater proportion of caregivers rated the severity of their children's problem behaviors to be within the Clinically Significant range than was expected in a normative population. Upon completion of the HOT DOCS program, caregivers' reported a statistically significant reduction in their perceptions of the severity of their target child's challenging behaviors as compared to perceptions prior to beginning the program. In terms of weekly progress monitoring of at-home skill use, participants' ratings of the ease or difficulty of use followed a similar pattern across each of the five skills. Specifically, participants reported a slight improvement in ease of use when their scores were averaged. The Tip Tracker's primary function is to serve as a self-monitoring tool for participants to remind them to use the skills they learned in class. Participants are encouraged to hang it in a visible and well-frequented area of their home such as the kitchen refrigerator to prompt them to use the skill and keep track of their behavior. The instrument has not been evaluated for reliability and validity and therefore at this time, data analyses are limited to visual and descriptive interpretations.

Participants indicated high levels of satisfaction with the HOT DOCS program, with the majority of participants indicating that the program met their expectations and provided useful skills and techniques. Most participants reported that they are using the specific parenting skills and problem solving techniques taught in the program; that they have shared the information they learned with family, friends, and/or co-workers; that they desired more time for instruction (e.g., more sessions, longer classes); and that they valued the knowledge and support from instructors and were encouraged by other caregivers struggling with situations similar to their own.

Discussion

Implications for Practitioners

The data support the potential effectiveness of the HOT DOCS parent training program as a form of early intervention for caregivers of children with challenging behaviors. Findings support the effectiveness of using this group-delivered parent training program to address early-emerging challenging behavior through problem-solving and skill enhancement. Results of the behavior rating scales suggest that participants perceived child behavior to be significantly less severe at post-test as compared to pre-test. Further, participants demonstrated a significant increase in knowledge of child development and strategies to address problem behaviors between pre- and post-test. Finally, the majority of participants endorsed positive outcomes such as learning strategies to implement with their children that they were able to use, and sharing the information they learned with others including important pediatric professionals like early interventionists, speech therapists, and pediatricians.

Furthermore, HOT DOCS has been made available to a large proportion of low socio-economic status (SES) families in the community because it is funded by a grant from the Children's Board of Hillsborough County. This funding covers the cost of the trainers' fees, materials, supplies and food for participants, as well as the participant registration fee, removing the financial barriers to participation in parent training programs identified by previous research (Barkley et al., 2000; Webster-Stratton & Taylor, 2001). By eliminating registration fees for families, access increases for all families who are willing and able to participate. Included in this sample were data from previously underserved portions of the population such as Hispanic or Spanish-speaking families and caregivers from low SES families, as defined by participant self-report. In fact, a disproportionately higher number of Hispanic or Latino families participated in HOT DOCS (37.7%) as compared with Hillsborough County, Florida 2006-2008 census data indicating that Hispanic or Latino families comprised 22% of the population (U.S. Census Bureau, n.d.).

Like other effective parenting programs, HOT DOCS provides a structured sequence of topics, which includes the use of empirical strategies such as praise, replacement behaviors, and limit setting, and provides explicit instruction to help caregivers determine which strategies work best for their child and family. The emphasis on the problem-solving method sets HOT DOCS apart from other parent training programs, which rely only on specific behavioral strategies, as this approach may be used to address both current and future challenges. The Tip Tracker is another unique addition to the HOT DOCS problem solving method, and was designed to help participants self-monitor their implementation of new skills. Progress monitoring is an assessment method that uses data to document small changes in behavior. This process is widely used in both educational and health interventions, and has been recognized as effective practice for over 20 years (Batsche et al., 2005). Given that there is currently no accepted standard for assessing parenting, this tool may be useful for future research testing parenting interventions (Scott, 2010).   Lastly, there is a detailed manual and training CD allowing others to replicate this approach, which may be used in both group and individual applications.

Limitations

Some limitations are acknowledged. First, HOT DOCS is a community-based project, which was developed to address the needs of young children, their families, and service providers, thus it did not follow the control-comparison group model. Further, a convenience sample of parents and caregivers referred for intervention due to their concerns with their child's behavior was utilized, which may not be representative of the true population. In addition, the underrepresentation of African American caregivers in the HOT DOCS program may pose a limitation in generalizing these results to some racial groups. The use of a non-standardized pre/post-test to gauge caregiver knowledge does not allow for comparison to other parenting programs. And finally, the evidence of effectiveness in child outcomes is limited to questionnaires completed by participants, and may not reflect true changes in behavior of either caregivers or children.

Future Directions

Future research on HOT DOCS should incorporate the use of a comparison or control group to strengthen evaluation findings. For example, caregivers on a waiting list could be asked to complete the HOT DOCS Knowledge Test and behavior rating scales (both pre-test and post-test) over a similar time interval as active participants while waiting to participate in the program. In order to increase the reliability and validity of findings related to caregiver knowledge, the HOT DOCS Knowledge Test is currently being refined and validated. To do so, Crocker and Algina's (1986) 10 steps of test construction are being utilized including identifying the construct of interest and initial item construction, followed by expert panel review to evaluate item content validity, pilot testing of items with a representative sample, item revision, and further testing to assess validity and reliability. Due to the developmental and ecological context of this research, it may be beneficial to collect longitudinal, follow-up data on the participants to contribute to the understanding of the long-term outcomes of early-emerging problem behaviors and early intervention strategies, particularly participation in the HOT DOCS parent training program and its effects on future academic and social behaviors of the target children and their families. Finally, direct observation of parenting would serve to document the effectiveness of HOT DOCS strategies on parenting and child outcomes.

Efforts to engage African American participation in HOT DOCS might include increased advertising in other community settings, such as churches and schools which serve these families. In addition, a cadre of parent trainers representing these communities could be trained as HOT DOCS coaches, who would then offer local trainings to families. This strategy was successfully employed by Armstrong, Hornbeck, Beam, Mack and Popkave (2006) in their implementation of the original edition of the HOT DOCS program, *Helping Our Toddlers (H.O.T.)*, during which time the curriculum was co-presented by a member of the H.O.T. team and the minister of an African-American church, and meetings were held in the church. As a result of this effort African-American participation in this set of classes reached 28%.

Conclusion

Preliminary data suggest improved outcomes for participants of the HOT DOCS program and their children and clients, including increases in caregiver knowledge, use of skills at home, high levels of satisfaction with the training, and reductions in the perceived severity of child behavior problems. In addition, several modifications were identified that could be made to the evaluation methodology to improve participant outcomes and increase the validity and reliability of program evaluations, including changes to measurement instruments (e.g., knowledge test, adaptive skill measure, evaluation survey, observations) and data collection procedures (e.g., waitlist control group, low rate of return of post-test rating scales). Overall, the HOT DOCS parent training program offers a promising early intervention approach that may be replicated in other community settings.

References

Achenbach, T. (2001). *Manual for the Achenbach system of empirically based assessment(ASEBA)*. Burlington, VT: University of Vermont, Research Center for Children, Youth, & Families.

Agazzi, H., Salinas, A., Williams, J., Chiriboga, D., Ortiz, C. & Armstrong, K. (2010). Adaptation of a behavioral parent training curriculum for Hispanic caregivers: HOT DOCS Español. *Infant Mental Health Journal, 32*, 182-200.

Armstrong, K., & Hornbeck, M. (2005). *Helping our Toddlers: Lessons for parents of young children with challenging behaviors*. Tampa, FL: University of South Florida, Louis de la Parte Florida Mental Health Institute, Department of Child and Family Studies.

Armstrong, K., Hornbeck, M., Beam, B., Mack, K., & Popkave, K. (2006). Evaluation of a curriculum for caregivers of young children with challenging behaviors. *Journal of Early Childhood and Infant Psychology, 2*, 51-61.

Armstrong, K., Lilly, C., & Curtiss, H. (2006). *Helping our toddlers, developing our children's skills*. Tampa, FL: University of South Florida, Department of Pediatrics, Division of Child Development.

Barkley, R., Shelton, T., Crosswait, C., Moorehouse, M., Fletcher, K., Barrett, S., et al. (2000). Multi-method psycho-educational intervention for preschool children with disruptive behavior: Preliminary results at post-treatment. *Journal of Child Psychology and Psychiatry, 3*, 319-322.

Batsche, G., Elliot, J., Graden, J., Grimes, J., Kovaleski, J., Prasse, D., et al. (2005). *Response to intervention*. Alexandria, VA: National Association of State Directors of Special Education.

Bronfenbrenner, U. (1979). *The ecology of human development: Experiments by nature and design*. Cambridge, MA: Harvard University Press.

Campbell, S. (1995). Behavior problems in preschool children: A review of recent research. *Journal of Child Psychology & Psychiatry & Allied Disciplines, 36*, 113-149.

Coie, J., & Dodge, K. (1998). Aggression and antisocial behavior. In W. Damon (Editor in Chief) & N. Eisenberg (Vol. Ed.), *Handbook of child psychology, 5th edition, Volume 3, Social, emotional, and personality development* (pp. 719-788). NY: John Wiley & Sons.

Crocker, L. & Algina, J. (1986). *Introduction to classical and modern test theory*. Orlando, FL: Holt, Rinehart and Winston.

Dishion, T., French, D., & Patterson, G. (1995). The development and ecology of antisocial behavior. In D. Cicchetti & D. J. Cohen (Eds.), *Developmental Psychopathology, Vol. 2: Risk, disorder, and adaptation* (pp. 421-471). New York: John Wiley & Sons.

Gross, D., Fogg, L., Webster-Stratton, C., Garvey, C., Julion, W., & Grady, J. (2003). Parent training of toddlers in day care in low-income urban communities. *Journal of Consulting & Clinical Psychology, 71*, 261-278.

Kazdin, A. (1993). Adolescent mental health: Prevention and treatment programs. *American Psychologist, 48*, 127-141.

Kazdin, A. (1995). Conduct disorder. In F. C. Verhulst & H. M. Koot (Eds.), *The epidemiology of child and adolescent psychopathology* (pp. 258-290). New York: Oxford University Press.

Kazdin, A., & Kendall, P. (1998). Current progress and future plans for developing effective treatments: Comments and perspectives. *Journal of Clinical Psychology, 27*, 217-226.

Keenan, K., & Wakschlag, L. (2000). More than the terrible twos: The nature and severity of behavior problems in clinic-referred preschool children. *Journal of Abnormal Child Psychology, 28*, 33-46.

Knapp, P., Ammen, S., Arstein-Kerslake, C., Poulsen, M., & Mastergeorge, A. (2007). Feasibility of expanding services for very young children in the public mental health setting. *Journal of the American Academy of Child and Adolescent Psychiatry, 46*, 152-161.

Knitzer, J. (2007). Putting knowledge into policy: Toward an infant-toddler policy agenda. *Infant Mental Health Journal, 28*, 237-245.

Lavigne, J., Gibbons, R., Christoffel, K. K., Arend, R., Rosenbaum, D., Binns, H., et al. (1996). Prevalence rates and correlates of psychiatric disorders among preschool children. *Journal of the American Academy of Child & Adolescent Psychiatry, 35*, 204-214.

Lundahl, B., Risser, H., & Lovejoy, C. (2006). A meta-analysis of parent training: Moderators and follow-up effects. *Clinical Psychology Review, 26*, 86-104.

Maughan, D., Christiansen, E., Jenson, W., Olympia, D., & Clark, E. (2005). Behavioral parent training as a treatment for externalizing behaviors and disruptive behavior disorders: A meta-analysis. *School Psychology Review, 34*, 267-286.

Nelson, C. (1995). A meta-analysis of parent education programs for children two to nine years. *Dissertation Abstracts International: Section B: The Sciences and Engineering, 56*, 1686.

Reid, J. (1993). Prevention of conduct disorder before and after school entry: Relating interventions to developmental findings. *Development and Psychopathology, 5*, 243-262.

Sandall, S., & Ostrosky, M. (Eds.). (1999). *Young exceptional children: Practical ideas for addressing challenging behaviors (1st ed.).* Denver, CO: Division for Early Childhood of the Council for Exceptional Children.

Sanders, M. (1999). Triple P-Positive Parenting Program: Towards an empirically validated multilevel parenting and family support strategy for the prevention of behavior and emotional problems in children. *Clinical Child and Family Psychology Review, 2*, 71-90.

Scott, S. (2010). National dissemination of effective parenting programmes to improve child outcomes. *The British Journal of Psychiatry, 196*, 1-3.

Skinner, B. (1953). *Science and human behavior*. New York, NY: Macmillan Free Press.

Smagner, J., & Sullivan, M. (2005). Investigating the effectiveness of behavioral parent training with involuntary clients in child welfare settings. *Research on Social Work Practice, 15*, 431-439.

Smith, B. J., & Fox, L. (2003, January). *Systems of Service Delivery: A Synthesis of Evidence Relevant to Young Children at Risk for or Who Have Challenging Behavior*. Retrieved September 21, 2006, from the Center for Evidence-Based Practice: Young Children with Challenging Behaviors website: http://challengingbehavior.fmhi.usf.edu/resources/smith-fox-jan03.pdf.

Sontag, J. (1996). Towards a comprehensive theoretical framework for disability research: Bronfenbrenner revisited. *Journal of Special Education, 3*, 319-344.

Tremblay, R. (2000). The development of aggressive behavior during childhood: What have we learned in the past century? *International Journal of Behavioral Development, 24*, 129-141.

U.S. Census Bureau. (n.d.). *State & county quickfacts: Hillsborough county, F.L.* Retrieved January 21, 2010 from http://quickfacts.census.gov.

Walker, H., Kavanaugh, K., Stiller, B., Golly, A., Severson, H., & Feil, E. (1998). First Step to Success: An early intervention approach for preventing school antisocial behavior. *Journal of Emotional and Behavioral Disorders, 6*, 66-80.

Webster-Stratton, C. (1998). Preventing conduct problems in Head Start children: Strengthening parenting competencies. *Journal of Consulting and Clinical Psychology, 66*, 715-730.

Webster-Stratton, C., & Taylor, T. (2001). Nipping early risk factors in the bud: Preventing substance abuse, delinquency, and violence in adolescence through interventions targeted at young children (0 to 8 Years). *Prevention Science, 2*, 165-192.

Review of the Battelle Developmental Inventory, Second Edition

Vincent C. Alfonso, Emily A. Rentz, & Suehee Chung
Fordham University

This article reviews the *Battelle Developmental Inventory-Second Edition* (BDI-2; Newborg, 2005a), a comprehensive assessment or screening tool of functional abilities of young children ages birth to 7 years, 11 months across five domains of development (i.e., Adaptive, Personal-Social, Communication, Motor, and Cognitive). The authors provide a brief overview of the BDI-2, discuss the administration and scoring procedures, and describe the test's materials. A critical evaluation of the technical adequacy of the instrument including standardization characteristics, reliability, test floors, item gradients, and validity is provided using the criteria set forth by Alfonso and Flanagan (2009). Finally, the BDI-2 Screening Test (ST) is briefly described, conclusions are drawn about the BDI-2, and recommendations are made regarding the use of the BDI-2 in practice. Given that the majority of the psychometric characteristics of the BDI-2 were rated positively (i.e., adequate to good), it is highly recommended for the assessment of young children's development, and represents an improvement over its predecessor.

The original *Battelle Developmental Inventory* (BDI) was published in 1984 based on the concept of milestones, which refer to certain skills and behaviors that children typically develop at specific time periods in their lives (Newborg, Stock, Wnek, Guidubaldi, & Svinicki, 1984). The BDI was designed to determine where on the developmental trajectory a child is functioning and consisted of five developmental domains: Adaptive, Personal-Social, Communication, Motor, and Cognitive. In 2005, the BDI-Second Edition (BDI-2) was published and includes the same five developmental domains as the original BDI (Newborg, 2005a).

This review and evaluation of the technical characteristics of the BDI-2 (Newborg, 2005a) was conducted using criteria set forth by Alfonso and Flanagan (2009). These criteria were determined after the authors reviewed 34 comprehensive descriptions, and reviews of, and criteria for evaluating norm-referenced instruments for preschoolers. Although their list of characteristics and

All correspondence should be addressed to Vincent C. Alfonso, Ph.D., Fordham University, Graduate School of Education, 113 West 60th Street, Room 1121, New York, NY 10023. Electronic mail may be sent to: alfonso@fordham.edu.

evaluative criteria is not exhaustive or inarguable (e.g., there are no criteria for test ceilings or standard error of measurement), we believe that for the most part, they are comprehensive and applicable to the BDI-2.[1] In the test review that follows, first we provide a brief overview of the BDI-2, discuss the administration and scoring procedures, and describe the test's materials. Next, we provide a critical evaluation of the technical adequacy of the instrument including standardization characteristics, reliability, test floors, item gradients, and validity. Finally, we briefly describe the BDI-2 Screener, draw some conclusions about the BDI-2, and make some recommendations regarding the use of the BDI-2 in practice.

Test Description

The BDI-2 (Newborg, 2005a) is a behaviorally based, individually administered, standardized assessment battery of developmental skills of children from birth through 7 years, 11 months of age. The BDI-2 is produced and distributed by the Riverside Publishing Company and is a revised version of the original BDI published in 1984 (Newborg et al.). The BDI-2 may be used as a comprehensive assessment or screening tool of functional abilities across five major domains of development (i.e., Adaptive, Personal-Social, Communication, Motor, and Cognitive). Each domain is comprised of either two or three subdomains. Table 1 provides the names and number of items for each BDI-2 domain and subdomain. Although the BDI-2 full battery consists of 450 items, only a subset of them is administered to a child based on the child's age range (Athanasiou, 2007). As reported in the administration manual, depending on the age of the child, the full battery can typically be administered between 1 and 1.5 hours. The Screening test has an administration time ranging from 10 to 30 minutes (Newborg, 2005b).

The standard applications of the BDI-2 include identifying current developmental levels, as well as strengths and learning opportunities of typically developing children and children with disabilities, as well as to assess infants and children considered to be "at-risk" for developmental delay (Newborg,

---

[1] The adequacy of the technical characteristics of preschool instruments has been investigated by a number of independent researchers (e.g., Alfonso & Flanagan, 1999; Bracken, 1987; Bracken, Keith, & Walker, 1998; Bradley-Johnson, 2001; Evans & Bradley-Johnson, 1988; Flanagan & Alfonso, 1995; Oades-Sese & Alfonso, 2003, 2008). While there has been a demand for improved technical adequacy of tests intended for preschool populations, there has also been a lack of agreed-upon criteria for evaluating many technical characteristics of tests such as standardization characteristics, reliability, and range of age divisions in norms tables. In 2009, Alfonso and Flanagan summarized the most salient psychometric criteria, comprehensive descriptions, and qualitative reviews of preschool instruments found in more than 30 publications. They concluded that not only did variability in criteria exist, but many investigators did not use any criteria in their evaluation of the instruments they reviewed. In an attempt to move toward a uniform set of criteria for evaluating adequacy of the technical characteristics of instruments for preschoolers, the authors provided a detailed description of technical characteristics as well as corresponding criteria and evaluative classifications that they believed were the most appropriate to incorporate in any review of preschool assessment instruments. These criteria and evaluative classifications can be found in Table 5.2 of Alfonso and Flanagan's 2009 chapter.

Table 1

Domains, Subdomains, and Number of Items on the Battelle Developmental Inventory-Second Edition

Domain (# of items)	Subdomain (# of items)
Adaptive (60)	Self-Care (35)
	Personal Responsibility (25)
Personal-Social (100)	Adult Interaction (30)
	Peer Interaction (25)
	Self-Concept and Social Role (45)
Communication (85)	Receptive (40)
	Expressive (45)
Motor (100)	Gross (45)
	Fine (30)
	Perceptual (25)
Cognitive (105)	Attention and Memory (30)
	Reasoning and Academic Skills (35)
	Perception and Concepts (40)

2005b). Additional uses of the BDI-2 include general screening of preschool and kindergarten children, developing individualized education programs, and monitoring student progress on short- and long-term bases. The BDI-2 is primarily designed for use by infant interventionists; preschool, kindergarten, and primary school teachers; and special educators. However, the BDI-2 is also often used by other professionals such as speech pathologists, school psychologists, and clinical diagnosticians (Newborg, 2005b).

The BDI-2 retained several important features from the original BDI and many of the subdomains and items from the first edition are found in the second edition. However, outdated items were deleted and new items were added to reflect more recent research findings related to cognitive development and to correspond better with early childhood curricula. Significant improvements were made in the psychometric design by repositioning test items in different domains or subdomains, collapsing and combining subdomains, revising the basal and ceiling rules, and adding items that measure skills more comprehensively at the low and high ends of the age ranges (Newborg, 2005b). Other improvements include an expanded normative sample and norm tables with smaller age ranges at all levels;

use of scaled, standard, percentile, and change sensitive scores for scoring and interpretation of results; simpler scoring procedures and clearer administration directions; more colorful and engaging pictures and manipulatives; and all items are now available in Spanish (Newborg, 2005b). The BDI-2 also makes use of new technology to facilitate administration, scoring, and report preparation. Professionals have the option of administering the BDI-2 via the *BDI-2 Data Buddie*™, a mobile electronic assistant that eliminates the need for paper record forms. In addition, Web-based and standalone computer software (i.e., the *BDI-2 Data Manager*) are available that provide a range of different reports (e.g., individual, class-, school-, and district-level) (Newborg, 2005b).

Administration and Scoring

According to Bliss (2007), starting points for each subdomain are determined by the child's chronological age and listed on the record form. There are three different administration procedures for the BDI-2: Structured, Observation, and Interview. One or more procedures are specified for every test item in each of the domain item books, with the preferred method listed first. The examiner must be familiar with each of these methods in order to determine when and when not to use a particular method. The examiner will have to use professional judgment when conflicting information is obtained from different sources to determine what accurately represents best the child's level of development. In the Structured procedure, the examiner obtains information by directly administering items to the child in a controlled, one-to-one setting. The Observation procedure evaluates skills that cannot be easily assessed via the Structured procedure, but should be used only when the examiner has opportunity to observe the child in his or her natural setting over an extended period of time. If the examiner has limited contact with the child, then the Interview procedure is recommended. In the Interview procedure, the examiner elicits information about a child's behavior from his or her parent, caregiver, or teacher in a face-to-face dialogue. A script for items using the Interview procedure is provided and usually the informant is required to supply examples of the behavior in question (Newborg, 2005b).

Regardless of the method of administration used, the items are subjected to an explicit 3-point objective scoring system which takes into account skills that are not exhibited by the child (score = 0), skills that are emerging (score = 1), and skills that are fully developed (score = 2). The basal and ceiling levels of functioning are determined using uniform rules of "three consecutive 2-point responses for basal and three [consecutive] 0-point responses for ceiling" (Bliss, 2007, p. 409). Raw scores for each subdomain are converted to scaled scores which are then added and the sum is converted to yield the domain standard scores (deviation quotients). Finally, the domain deviation quotients are summed and that sum is converted to the BDI-2 total score (Bliss, 2007).

Materials

The BDI-2 materials include an examiner's manual, an item test book for each of the five domains and the screening test, comprehensive battery and screening record forms, a student workbook for select items at the upper ages, comprehensive battery and screening stimulus books, presentation cards, and a plastic puzzle/strip sheet (Newborg, 2005b). Manipulative kits are available separately in either complete or specialized sets offering only the unique or difficult to find items, such as a shoe, blue cubes, and stackable rings (Athanasiou, 2007). A complete list of required manipulatives and those offered in the specialized set is found on page 21 of the examiner's manual (Newborg, 2005b). As indicated above, a Web-based computer-scoring service, an independent computer-scoring software program, and an electronic mobile assistant package are available for separate purchase as well. Translated/adapted materials in Spanish are also available but "normative information applies only when direct assessment items are presented in English" (Barton & Spiker, 2007, p. 68).

Technical Adequacy

The review of technical adequacy of the BDI-2 follows the criteria set forth by Alfonso and Flanagan (2009). For most psychometric properties, there are three evaluative classifications: *Good, Adequate,* and *Inadequate.* Specific criteria for each classification are listed in a user friendly table in Alfonso and Flanagan (2009, pp. 146-148).

Standardization

The standardization sample of the BDI-2 included 2,500 children ages birth through 7 years, 11 months, with 125 children in each of 20 age groups (children ages 0 to 23 months were grouped into 3-month age groups, and children ages 24 to 95 months were grouped into 6-month age groups). Because there were at least 2,000 individuals overall and at least 200 individuals per 1-year interval, the size of the normative group and number of individuals at each 1-year age interval for the BDI-2 was rated *Good.* Normative data were collected over a 14-month period in 2002 and 2003 and thus this characteristic (i.e., recency of normative data) was rated *Good* as well. The norm tables for individuals birth to 23 months are provided in 1-month intervals, resulting in a rating of *Good*, while the norm tables for children 24 months and older are provided in three-month intervals, resulting in a rating of *Adequate.*

The standardization sample of the BDI-2 closely matched the percentages of age, sex, race/ethnicity, geographic region, and socioeconomic (SES) levels as reported by the U.S. Census Bureau (2001, cited in Newborg, 2005b). However, mother's educational attainment was the only variable used to represent SES level as other indicators, such as occupation and income, were viewed as "problematic" (Newborg, 2005b, p. 100) or "too complex" (Newborg, 2005b, p. 101) to use. Children with acute medical conditions, marked sensory or communication deficits, or severe behavioral or emotional disturbances were not included in the normative sample. Nevertheless, the match of the demographic characteristics of the normative group to the U.S. population with SES included was rated *Good*. Overall, the adequacy of the standardization sample of the BDI-2 was rated *Good*, even though one standardization characteristic was rated *Adequate* (i.e., norm table age divisions for 24-95 months are provided in 3-month intervals).

Evaluation of BDI-2 Reliability

Internal consistency. According to the *Standards for Educational and Psychological Testing* (*Standards*; American Educational Research Association [AERA], American Psychological Association [APA], & National Council on Measurement in Education [NCME], 1999), internal consistency refers to the reliability of correlations among different items on the same test, measuring with what level of certainty different items are measuring the same construct. Internal consistency reliability coefficients for the 13 subdomain scaled scores, 5 domain Deviation Quotients (DQ), and Total Score DQ for each of the sixteen 6-month age groups from the BDI-2 standardization sample are provided in the test manual (Newborg, 2005b). In addition, average internal consistency reliability coefficients across all age groups are provided. Coefficients for the 13 subdomain scaled scores were calculated using the split-half method and corrected with the Spearman-Brown formula (Newborg, 2005b).

The Total Score DQ internal consistency coefficients were rated *Good* across the age range of the test. That is, each coefficient is ≥ .90. The internal consistency coefficients for the five BDI-2 domain DQs were rated primarily *Good* or *Adequate*. That is, 99% of the coefficients (79/80) were ≥ .80. Only 1% of the domain DQ internal reliability coefficients (1/80) was rated as *Inadequate* (i.e., Adaptive Domain at 12-17 months), as the coefficient was < .80.

The BDI-2 manual (Newborg, 2005b) also provides the internal consistency reliability coefficients for all subdomains at all applicable ages. Of the 168 coefficients reported on page 110 in the manual, 89% or 150/168 were rated as *Good* or *Adequate* (i.e., ≥ .80). Only 11% or 18/168 of the subdomain internal consistency coefficients were rated as *Inadequate* because they are < .80.

Test-retest stability. The BDI-2 manual (Newborg, 2005b) reports a study of two age groups consisting of 126 two-year-olds and 126 four-year-olds who were administered the BDI-2 on two occasions by the same examiner. The age range of the test-retest groups or samples did not span more than a one-year interval and thus was rated *Good*. Because each test-retest sample consisted of at least 50 individuals and represented the U.S. population on at least three demographic variables (i.e., sex, race/ethnicity, and SES) the size and representativeness of these samples was rated as *Adequate*. Testing intervals ranged from 2 to 25 days, with a median retest interval of 8 days. Thus, the length of the test-retest interval was rated as *Good* (i.e., ≤ 3 months). Finally, the test-retest reliability coefficients for all BDI-2 domains and total score DQs across the two samples were rated *Good* or *Adequate* (≥ .80); whereas 85% (22/26) of test-retest reliability coefficients for all BDI-2 subdomain scaled scores across the two samples were rated as *Adequate* and 15% (4/26) were rated as *Inadequate*.

Overall, the test-retest reliability of the BDI-2 is exemplary given the sampling, length of the test-retest interval, and magnitude of the reliability coefficients. Additional test-retest samples of different ages such as individuals younger than 2 years of age and older than 4 years of age are necessary to demonstrate that the BDI-2 is a reliable instrument over time across the entire age range of the test.

Evaluation of BDI-2 Test Floors

In general, the BDI-2 subdomains have *Adequate* floors.[2] For example, with rare exception practitioners are able to discriminate effectively among various degrees of functioning at the lower extremes of the ability continuum. These rare exceptions occur at 2 months and below for many of the BDI-2 subdomains. All BDI-2 domain and total score DQs have *Adequate* floors across the age range of the test. Overall, the test floors for the BDI-2 subdomains, domains, and total score were rated *Adequate*.

Evaluation of BDI-2 Item Gradients

The item gradients for all BDI-2 subdomains across the age range of the test (i.e., 0-95 months) were rated *Good*. That is, there are no item gradient violations[3] as per the criteria set forth by Alfonso and Flanagan (2009).

Evaluation of BDI-2 Validity

Although the BDI-2 manual (Newborg, 2005b) refers to the validity framework proposed in the *Standards* (AERA et al., 1999), the BDI-2 validity evidence is organized and discussed according to the more traditional concepts of content, criterion, and construct validity evidence. In this review and evaluation

---

[2] Test floors can be either Adequate or Inadequate. No other rating is applicable for this test characteristic (Alfonso & Flanagan, 2009).

[3] Item gradient refers to the density of items across a test's latent trait scale. A test with good item gradient characteristics has items that are approximately equally spaced in difficulty along the entire scale of the test, and the distance between items is small enough to allow for reliable discrimination between individuals on the latent trait measured by the test (McGrew & Flanagan, 1998). Item gradient information is concerned with the extent to which changes in a single raw score point on a test result in excessively large changes in ability scores (or standard scores; Bracken, 1987). The interested reader may want to review Alfonso and Flanagan (2009, pp. 150-152) for greater details regarding item gradient violations and a system for evaluating this test characteristic.

of the BDI-2 validity evidence, we adhere to the five major strands of validity discussed in the *Standards*: test content, response processes, internal structure, relations to other variables, and consequences of testing.

Evidence based on test content. Validity evidence based on test content "refers to the themes, wording, and format of its items and tasks, as well as guidelines for procedures regarding administration and scoring" (AERA et al., 1999, p. 11). A description of the BDI-2 test development and standardization process is provided on pages 95-108 in the examiner's manual (Newborg, 2005b). Details regarding each of the five major stages in the 5-year development of the BDI-2 including planning, field testing of new items, tryout edition, standardization edition, and final published edition are provided in a very thorough, clear, and explicit manner. The names of the trainers, project recruiters, data quality assurance managers, and examiners who participated in the standardization of the BDI-2 are provided in Appendix G of the examiner's manual (Newborg, 2005b). The names of the institutions that participated in the standardization, research, and tryout studies are found in Appendix H of the examiner's manual (Newborg, 2005b). Moreover, details regarding literature reviews, expert advice, user surveys, field testing of new items, tryout edition study, scoring studies, item fairness studies, and complete design of the standardization edition and final published edition are available. A thorough treatment of administration and scoring of the BDI-2 is provided in the examiner's manual (Newborg, 2005b, pp. 43-64).

Newborg (2005b) discusses evidence of test content validity via professional judgment of content, coverage of important constructs, and empirical item analysis. Regarding *professional judgment of content*, Newborg states "Hundreds of professional examiners reviewed every item in the Tryout and Standardization Editions, completing comprehensive questionnaires stating their concerns about items and subdomains" (p. 117). Specific details regarding item development, fairness, and selection are found in Chapter 6 of the examiner's manual (Newborg, 2005b, pp. 95-108).

In the section on *coverage of important constructs*, Newborg (2005b) discusses that experts in child development were asked to rate the original BDI items according to the developmental domain being assessed. The "items were classified into comprehensive lists for each domain. These lists proved valuable in creating early versions of new items and new subdomains" (Newborg, 2005b, p. 117). As a result, the structure of the BDI-2 consists of 5 domains and 13 subdomains "central to child-development theory" (Newborg, 2005b, p. 117).

Finally, *empirical item analysis* was used to provide evidence of BDI-2 test content validity. These analyses included item discrimination, percent correct at successive age levels, a number of model-data-fit-statistics, and differential item functioning. According to Newborg, "All of these analyses and item studies created homogeneous, unifactor scales having consistent evidence of model-data fit and content relevance" (2005b, p. 117).

Overall, the test content validity evidence of the BDI-2 is notable. The treatment of test development and standardization is comprehensive and reader friendly and extensive details regarding item development, placement, and fit are provided throughout the examiner's manual (Newborg, 2005b).

Evidence based on response processes. According to the *Standards* (AERA et al., 1999), this strand of validity evidence provides support regarding "the fit between the construct and the detailed nature of performance or response actually engaged in by examinees" (p. 12). This strand of validity evidence is not addressed in the BDI-2 manual and thus could not be evaluated directly. In addition, this strand of validity evidence may be especially difficult to demonstrate given that young children may not be able to explain sufficiently how they approach or solve tasks. The BDI-2 manual and item books do, however, provide details regarding item stimuli, item requirements, and item response modalities that are very helpful to examiners and perhaps to children. This information reflects some evidence of response processes because it makes clear what is expected of examiners and the children they assess.

We also suggest that examiners attend closely to young children's responses to test items, test stimuli, and the test environment so that accurate (valid) interpretations of their performance can be made. For example, young children's reactions to test items such as laughing, demonstrating frustration, or turning away from the examiner may suggest difficulties with the test itself rather than a possible developmental delay (Alfonso, Russo, Fortugno, & Rader, 2005). In addition, if the examiner is able to collect information about the child's interests and responses to situations via parent, caregiver, or teacher interviews prior to the evaluation, he/she may be able to observe whether the child has the skills or abilities being measured using other materials or while completing other types of tasks. Careful observation of the child's responses when presented with stimuli may inform the examiner whether the elicited response is due to developmental delay or lack of interest. If the examiner believes the child's response is due to lack of interest, it may be beneficial to attempt another task measuring the same abilities and skills or make further inquiries regarding the child's behaviors when approached with similar situations (Alfonso et al.).[4]

Evidence based on internal structure. Validity evidence based on a test's internal structure refers to the "relationships among test items and test components that conform to the construct on which the proposed test score interpretations are based" (AERA et al., 1999, p. 13). Internal structure validity evidence for the BDI-2 includes analysis of growth curves; intercorrelations of the subdomain, domain, and total DQ scores; and exploratory and confirmatory factor analyses.

---

[4] We are not suggesting that examiners replace test items with their own items and score those responses that are correct. Rather, we are suggesting that examiners test the limits with young children by administering similar items after the complete test has been administered so that additional information may be garnered about the child's abilities. This information can be of great assistance in educational planning and can be shared with parents and teachers, alike.

Newborg provides evidence that the BDI-2 measures developmental growth by referring to the norms tables that show "the expected trend of increasing mean raw scores (located at scaled scores of 10 for subtests) through the birth to 7 years, 11 months age range" (2005b, p. 133). In addition, Newborg discusses and provides growth curves for the five BDI-2 domain scores. In general, these growth curves appear to be consistent with those found on other developmental tests and on age-related changes for various developmental domains of cognitive abilities (e.g., *Peabody Developmental Motor Scales-2*; Folio & Fewell, 2000; and *Developmental Indicators for the Assessment of Learning-3*; Mardell-Czudnowski & Goldenberg, 1998).

Intercorrelations of the subdomain scale scores, domain, and total DQ scores for three age groups (birth to 1 year, 11 months; 2 to 5 years; and 6 to 7 years) are provided in the BDI-2 examiner's manual (Newborg, 2005b, pp. 135-137). Inspection of these tables indicated that, in general, the patterns of correlations are consistent with developmental and psychometric theory. For example, 90% of the correlations between the domain scores ranged from .3 to .7. In addition, most subdomain scores are more highly correlated with their respective domain total scores than with other domain total scores and most correlations are higher among subdomains within a domain than with subdomains from other domains.

Various factor analyses (i.e., exploratory and confirmatory) are conducted as measures of internal reliability to determine "factors" or groupings of items that measure the same construct and to reduce the testing items in relevant groupings (i.e., subsets) of items (AERA et al., 1999). Regarding exploratory and confirmatory factor analyses, the standardization sample was divided into four age groups (i.e., < 24 months, 24-47 months, 48-71 months, and ≥ 72 months). All groups consisted of 500 individuals save the first group that consisted of 1,000 individuals. The exploratory factor analysis (EFA) used standardized half scores and a principal axis (common) factor analysis using least squares estimation followed by oblique (promax) rotation to explore factor solutions for each age group. According to Newborg (2005b), five clearly defined factor solutions were determined and the oblique rotation provided factor correlations that ranged from .53 to .70 for the youngest age group (i.e., < 24 months) and .15 to .71 for the oldest group (≥ 72 months). Inspection of the factor loadings for the youngest and oldest age groups indicated that, for the most part, standardized half scores loaded highly on their appropriate domain (range = .23 - .99). However, factor loadings below .20 are not provided for these two age groups and no data are provided for inspection for the other two age groups.

Confirmatory factor analyses (CFA) were conducted for the same four age groups using covariance matrices with a maximum likelihood estimation for each model. Four models were compared using split-half subdomain scores: a) a one-factor model where all split-half scores were loaded on one general factor; b) a three-factor model with Adaptive and Personal-Social Domains as one factor,

Cognitive and Communication Domains as one factor, and the Motor Domain as the third factor; c) a four-factor model with the Adaptive and Personal-Social Domain as one factor and the Cognitive, Communication, and Motor Domains as separate factors; and d) a five-factor model where the Personal Responsibility and Self-Care subdomains were loaded on the adaptive factor; the Peer Interaction, Adult Interaction, and Self-Concept and Social Role subdomains were loaded on the personal-social factor; the Perception and Concepts, Reasoning and Academic Skills, and Attention and Memory subdomains were loaded on the cognitive factor; the Expressive and Receptive Communication subdomains were loaded on the communication factor; and lastly, the Gross, Fine, and Perceptual Motor subdomains were loaded on the motor factor.

Several goodness of fit indices including chi-square, root mean squared error of approximation, the standardized root mean square residual, and the non-normed fit index were used to examine the fit of the four hypothesized factor models. According to Newborg (2005b), the best fit to the data for 2- to 3-year-old-children and 4- to 5-year-old children was the five-factor model. Inspection of factor loadings for these two age groups indicated that all loadings exceeded .40 with a range of .46 to .88. Once again, however, factor loadings below .20 are not provided for these two age groups and no data are provided for inspection for the other two age groups.

Similar to the content validity evidence discussed above, the construct validity evidence for the BDI-2 is impressive overall. Growth curves, intercorrelations among domains and subdomains, and factor analyses provide ample evidence for the construct validity of the BDI-2. However, the author is remiss in not providing all factor loadings for all age groups.

Evidence based on relations to other variables. The relationship between external variables and internal variables informs criterion-related validity as there are expected relationships between scales hypothesized to measure the same constructs (concurrent validity) as well as anticipated relationships between scales with related and different constructs (convergent & divergent validity, respectively) (AERA et al., 1999). The BDI-2 manual (Newborg, 2005b) contains detailed information regarding the relationship of the BDI-2 to tests that measure similar and different constructs. These tests include the BDI (Newborg et al., 1984); the *Bayley Scales of Infant Development, Second Edition* (BSID-2; Bayley, 1993); the *Denver Developmental Screening Test-II* (DDST-II; Frankenburg et al., 1992); the *Preschool Language Scale, Fourth Edition* (PLS-4; Zimmerman, Steiner, & Pond, 2002); the *Vineland Social-Emotional Early Childhood Scales* (Vineland SEEC; Sparrow, Balla, & Cicchetti, 1998); the *Comprehensive Test of Phonological Processing* (CTOPP; Wagner, Torgesen, & Rashotte, 1999); the *Wechsler Preschool and Primary Scale of Intelligence, Third Edition* (WPPSI™-III; Wechsler, 2002); and the *Woodcock-Johnson III Tests of Achievement* (WJ III ACH; Woodcock, McGrew, & Mather, 2001).

The first study reviewed here compared the original BDI to the BDI-2. One hundred ninety-one individuals were tested using a counterbalanced design with random assignment so that about half the sample was tested with the BDI first and the other half tested with the BDI-2 first. The sample was 49% female, consisted of children from birth to 6 years of age, and varied according to racial/ethnic backgrounds and maternal education. The correlation between the two BDI total scores was .78 and all correlations between the same domain scores were high (range = .64 to .76) and greater than correlations between different domain scores.

Studies with other developmental scales such as the BSID-2, DDST-II, PLS-4, and Vineland SEEC provided additional criterion-related validity evidence for the BDI-2. Sample characteristics such as number of participants, percentages of males and females, percentages of racial/ethnic backgrounds, and percentages of maternal education varied across studies. Details regarding these sample characteristics are found in the examiner's manual (Newborg, 2005b). In general, results of these studies support the BDI-2 as a test of young children's development. For example, the BDI-2 Cognitive and Communication domain scores correlated .61 and .75, respectively with the BSID-2 Mental Index, whereas the BDI-2 Motor domain score correlated .64 with the BSID-2 Motor Index demonstrating convergent validity. Lower correlations between the BDI-2 Cognitive and Communication domain scores and the BSID-2 Motor Index (.34 and .43, respectively) and between the BDI-2 Motor domain score and BSID-2 Mental Index (.48) demonstrated divergent validity.

In the study between the BDI-2 and DDST-II, percentage of classification agreement across four developmental domains was used to demonstrate convergent validity. The percentage of agreement between BDI-2 scores divided into two categories (> 1 standard deviation below the mean and < 1 standard deviation below the mean) and the Normal and Suspect categories of the DDST-II ranged from 83% to 90% with a median of 89%. According to Newborg (2005b), "These results indicate a high level of agreement between the BDI-2 scores and the DDST-II categories" (p. 121).

Additional convergent validity evidence is demonstrated using the PLS-4, a frequently administered standardized language test for young children. For example, the BDI-2 Communication DQ and the PLS-4 Total Language Standard Score were nearly the same (< 2 standard score points difference) and the BDI-2 Expressive scaled scores and PLS-4 Expressive standard scores correlated .73. Divergent validity was demonstrated by the .37 correlation between the BDI-2 Receptive scaled score and the PLS-4 Expressive standard score.

Finally, the last study conducted with a developmental scale that Newborg (2005b) reports was between the BDI-2 and Vineland SEEC, a standardized adaptive behavior measure for young children. Although some correlations between the BDI-2 Domain and Subdomain Scores and Vineland SEEC scores were not supportive of convergent and divergent validity evidence for the BDI-2, most correlations ranged between .50 and .69, reflecting common constructs between the BDI-2 and the Vineland SEEC. The highest correlations were between the BDI-2 Personal Responsibility subdomain and the Vineland SEEC Interpersonal Domain (.73) and between the BDI-2 Adaptive Domain and the Vineland SEEC Interpersonal Domain (.71) (Newborg, 2005b).

Newborg (2005b) also reports on studies between the BDI-2 and the CTOPP, WPPSI-III, and WJ III ACH. The study between the BDI-2 and CTOPP is not particularly useful given a small number of participants (i.e., 18) and that the BDI-2 does not directly assess any of the same constructs as the CTOPP. In the study between the BDI-2 and WPPSI-III Newborg indicates that the Cognitive Domain DQ correlated .75 with the WPPSI-III FSIQ, the highest among the nine correlations obtained. In addition, the Motor Domain DQ correlated .50 with the Performance IQ and only .39 with the Verbal IQ, an expected pattern given the constructs examined. As with the study conducted between the BDI-2 and CTOPP, the study between the BDI-2 and WJ III ACH produced limited supportive evidence for the BDI-2 because the BDI-2 includes only one subdomain comprised of academic tasks. Nevertheless, 42 participants were included in the study and of the 28 correlations obtained, the two highest occurred between the Cognitive Domain DQ and the Reasoning and Academic Skills subdomain of the BDI-2 and Pre-Academic standard scores of the WJ III ACH (.61 and .64, respectively). Several low correlations were reported between the Perception and Concepts subdomain of the BDI-2 and WJ III ACH subtest and cluster standard scores demonstrating divergent validity (Newborg, 2005b).

Evidence based on test consequences. Test developers and publishers are required to provide evidence that scores on their test result in accurate and appropriate decisions and classifications. In other words, scores on tests and decisions made based on them produce the intended consequences (AERA et al., 1999). Newborg (2005b) does not discuss this strand of validity directly, nor does she provide information on treatment/utility studies. She does, however, provide details of studies with individuals from the following exceptional or special groups: autism, cognitive delays, developmental delays, motor delays, prematurity, and speech and language delays. Interestingly, there was no group of children with intellectual disability in these special group studies. The studies reported by Newborg (2005b) were used to demonstrate the utility of the BDI-2 in classifying children according to special or clinical groups and thus provide some validity evidence based on the consequences of testing. Newborg compared groups of demographically matched typically developing children from the standardization sample to samples with individuals from each of the aforementioned special groups. Although the author provides demographic information about the special groups such as age, sex, and race/ethnicity, she does not provide any information regarding how the children in the special groups were located, diagnosed, or selected for the studies. This information is needed in order to make sound judgments regarding the results of these special group studies and to draw conclusions about the discriminant validity of the BDI-2.

Nevertheless, some comments can be made regarding the results of these special group studies. For example, all total standard scores for all special groups were between one and two standard deviations below the mean indicating that the BDI-2 does discriminate between atypically developing children and normally developing children since all groups of typically developing children earned total standard scores ≥ 97. Moreover, many of the special groups earned several domain standard scores between one and two standard deviations below the mean whereas the demographically matched children from the standardization sample earned domain standard scores ≥ 95. Again, the BDI-2 clearly discriminates special or clinical groups from normal or typical groups of children. However, that is where the discriminating power of the BDI-2 seems to end. A careful review of all domain standard scores for all special groups indicated that there is virtually no way to distinguish between the special groups based on BDI-2 domain standard scores. In other words, for example, even the most astute clinician or psychometrician could not discriminate between children in the autism group from children in the cognitively delayed groups because their group profiles of domain standard scores are nearly identical. Similar examples can be found simply by reviewing the mean domain standard scores for all special groups.

After the presentation of special group studies, Newborg (2005b) provides classification accuracy of the BDI-2 domain and total DQ scores. Sensitivity and specificity values were reported for the special groups either by domain or total DQ scores, or both. The sensitivity values ranged from a low of 0.75 for the motor delay group on the Motor DQ to a high of 0.93 for the cognitive delay group on the Cognitive Domain DQ. The specificity values ranged from a low of 0.75 for the speech and language delay group on the Communication DQ to a high of 0.91 for the autistic delay group on the Personal-Social DQ and the BDI-2 Total DQ. Detailed information regarding BDI-2 classification analyses are provided in the administration manual on pages 130-133 (Newborg, 2005b). Although the various accuracy values across the groups are impressive, once again these data demonstrate that the BDI-2 classifies children well as either atypically or typically developing. The BDI-2 cannot and should not be used to discriminate among various atypically developing groups of children and thus should not be used in isolation to diagnose children as having a particular developmental delay or disorder (Newborg, 2005b). The BDI-2 is not alone regarding discriminant validity as most developmental and cognitive tests do not discriminate among special or clinical groups and cannot be used for specific diagnoses save intellectual disability (as long as there is concomitant low functioning in adaptive behavior) (Alfonso & Flanagan, 2007; Kaufman, Flanagan, Alfonso, & Mascolo, 2006). Most recently, however, Matson, Mahan, Hess, and Fodstad (2010) used the DQ from the BDI-2 as the independent variable in a study with 198 toddlers with Autism Spectrum Disorders. Thus, independent researchers are using the BDI-2 in their research.

Our overall rating of the BDI-2 validity evidence presented in the manual (Newborg, 2005b) is *Adequate* to *Good* as per Alfonso and Flanagan (2009). For example, Newborg demonstrates that the BDI-2 is a measure of young children's development in several domains via careful and thorough item development, generally supportive factor analytic results, high intercorrelations among the BDI-2 domains and subdomains, special group difference data, and relations with measures of similar and dissimilar constructs that are significant and in the expected direction. Relatively weaker validity evidence is provided with respect to response processes and the consequences of testing, a finding that is common with other instruments designed to assess young children's functioning (Alfonso et al., 2005; Alfonso & Flanagan, 2009).

Although we have rated the BDI-2 validity evidence as *Adequate* to *Good*, additional research should be conducted to replicate findings in general and expand upon the data for special groups. Data should also be collected pre- and post-treatment for a variety of interventions to determine the treatment/utility of the BDI-2.

BDI-2 Screening Test (ST)

The purpose of the BDI-2 ST is to identify children who are at-risk or are already showing a developmental delay or disability and may need to be referred for a comprehensive evaluation. The BDI-2 ST is an abbreviated instrument that consists of 100 items (20 items per domain) from the comprehensive BDI-2. The BDI-2 ST materials include the following: the BDI-2 ST Item Test Book, 30 ST Record Forms, a ST Worksheet blackline master, a set of ST Presentation Cards with a small storage box, and a ST Stimulus Book. All ST materials are components of the comprehensive BDI-2. Administration time for children under the age of 3 years or over 5 years is estimated to be 10-15 minutes. For children between 3 and 5 years of age, administration time is approximately 20-30 minutes (Newborg, 2005b). Unlike the BDI-2 comprehensive assessment, the ST raw scores are not converted to standard scores or percentile ranks. Rather, cutoff scores are used for the five domains and the total score. A cutoff level may be 1.0, 1.5, or 2.0 standard deviations below the mean. An age equivalent for the total score can also be determined. The manual details various ways to make referral decisions for further evaluation based on the cutoff scores. Appendix E in the manual details the ST cutoff scores for each of the domains and age groups (Newborg, 2005b).

As the 100 ST items were selected from the finalized BDI-2 items, item development procedures and validity of the ST items are the same as the comprehensive BDI-2. Two items from each domain were selected for each age level. The items selected were those regarded as representing the most important milestone, having high item-total score correlations (.70 or higher), and having an item difficulty of approximately .75 (Newborg, 2005b). The reliability coefficients of the BDI-2 Total Screening Score range from .78 (90-95 months) to .96 (30-35 months), with an average reliability coefficient of .91 (Newborg, 2005b).

Through our assessment training facility for school psychology graduate students, the BDI-2 ST was administered to kindergarten students enrolled in several parochial schools in the New York City boroughs. School and counseling psychology graduate students were trained in the administration of the BDI-2 ST and in the assessment of young children and were closely supervised. Screening occurred in the fall of 2007 and 2008 with approximately 200 children screened each year. As reported in the BDI-2 manual (Newborg, 2005b), the materials (i.e., toys) proved to be very child-friendly and attractive. However, using and maintaining the manipulatives in an organized manner (during testing) was challenging for the examiners. Even with the screening test, utilization of the manipulatives kit is highly recommended.

Overall, the BDI-2 ST was found to be straightforward with regards to administration and scoring. The directions were clear and the scoring procedure was simple. However, although multiple data sources provide a more comprehensive assessment of skills, in three of the domains (Adaptive, Personal-Social, and Communication), the different types of administration (i.e., Structured, Interview, and Observation) were not generally separated from each other. That is, Interview items were embedded between Structured items or vice versa. This potentially complicates administration. For example, when administering Structured items (i.e., direct testing), the examiner may need to be more vigilant or more cautious in determining basal and ceiling levels since the item(s) in question may not be obtained via the Structured procedure, but need to be acquired through an Interview procedure. In order to establish basal and ceiling levels of functioning during a direct assessment, examiners may need to administer additional items or further question a parent/teacher at a later time if they are not present during testing of the child. This can add to the length of time for administration and may delay the completion of the assessment if the parent/teacher is not readily available for more questioning.

Nevertheless, our overall experience with the BDI-2 ST was positive. The results provide a good indication of a child's skill level and utilizing this test on an individual basis would pose very minimal complications, if any (for an experienced examiner). Conversely, this measure may not be optimal to use as a general screener in testing an entire class, unless the teacher is the examiner. Since the teacher is needed for interview on several items, it would be unreasonable to ask one teacher the same questions for 20 or more children. In our testing, we reviewed each interview item with the teachers, but asked them to name the child(ren) that had not demonstrated the skill or had shown difficulty with it. In a recent study published by D'Angiulli and Sullivan (2010) the BDI-2 ST was found to be a useful tool in determining the cognitive and social development of 22 prenatally substance-exposed infants in foster care homes. Thus, in general, the BDI-2 ST appears to be a reliable and valid screener for use with young children.

Conclusions and Recommendations for Practice

Overall, the BDI-2 is a substantial improvement over its predecessor for assessing the various capabilities of young children ages birth to 7 years, 11 months. As Athanasiou (2007) states, "The BDI-2 is a comprehensive, relatively user-friendly, and overall technically adequate measure of early childhood development" (p. 65). We could not agree more and believe that the BDI-2 is an exemplary instrument for the assessment of young children's development.

Nevertheless, the BDI-2 is not without limitations such as some areas of limited validity evidence, at times cumbersome administration and scoring procedures, and some software program concerns. With these limitations and our experience with the BDI-2, we suggest the following recommendations when using this instrument. First, examiners not accustomed to working with young children are advised to read Bracken's (2007) chapter for helpful hints on what to expect from and how to test young children. Second, examiners should become familiar with the BDI-2 administration and scoring procedures by practicing with colleagues and/or young children. Third, a thorough read of the BDI-2 manual (Newborg, 2005b) is strongly suggested so that examiners may understand better the technical limitations and subtle and not so subtle challenges in working with this instrument. Finally, as with any instrument for young children the BDI-2 may not be suitable for all children from all cultures and language backgrounds. Careful consideration of the BDI-2 quantitative and qualitative characteristics is strongly recommended prior to using it with a specific sample of children.

References

Alfonso, V. C., & Flanagan, D. P. (1999). Assessment of cognitive functioning in preschoolers. In E. V. Nuttall, I. Romero, & J. Kelesnik (Eds.), *Assessing and screening preschoolers* (2nd ed., pp. 186-217). Boston, MA: Allyn & Bacon.

Alfonso, V. C., & Flanagan, D. P. (2007). Best practices in the use of the Stanford-Binet Intelligence Scales, Fifth Edition (SB5) with preschoolers. In B. A. Bracken & R. Nagle (Eds.), P*sychoeducational assessment of preschool children* (4th ed., pp. 267-295). Mahwah, NJ: Erlbaum.

Alfonso, V. C., & Flanagan, D. P. (2009). Assessment of preschool children. In B.A. Mowder, F. Rubinson, & A. E. Yasik (Eds.), *Evidence-based practice in infant and early childhood psychology* (pp. 129-166). New York, NY: John Wiley and Sons.

Alfonso, V. C., Russo, P. M., Fortugno, D. A., & Rader, D. E. (2005, Spring). Critical review of the Bayley Scales of Infant Development-Second Edition: Implications for assessing young children with developmental delays. *The School Psychologist, 59,* 67-73.

American Educational Research Association, American Psychological Association, & National Council on Measurement in Education [AERA, APA, & NCME]. (1999). *Standards for educational and psychological testing.* Washington, DC: AERA.

Athanasiou, M. (2007). Review of the Battelle Developmental Inventory, 2nd Edition. In K. F. Geisinger, R. A. Spies, J. F. Carlson, & B. S. Plake (Eds.), *The seventeenth mental measurements yearbook* (pp. 63-65). Lincoln, NE: Buros Institute of Mental Measurement.

Barton, L. R., & Spiker, D. (2007). Review of the Battelle Developmental Inventory, 2nd Edition. In K. F. Geisinger, R. A. Spies, J. F. Carlson, & B. S. Plake (Eds.), *The seventeenth mental measurements yearbook* (pp. 66-71). Lincoln, NE: Buros Institute of Mental Measurement.

Bayley, N. (1993). *Bayley Scales of Infant Development, Second Edition.* (BSID-2). San Antonio, TX: Psychological Corporation.

Bliss, S. (2007). Test Reviews: Newborg, J. (2005) Battelle Developmental Inventory, Second Edition, Itasca, IL: Riverside Publishing. *Journal of Psychoeducational Assessment, 25*(4), 409-415.

Bracken, B. A. (1987). Limitations of preschool instruments and standards for minimal level of technical adequacy. *Journal of Psychoeducational Assessment, 4,* 313-326.

Bracken, B. A. (2007). Creating the optimal preschool testing situation. In B. A. Bracken & R. Nagle (Eds.), Psychoeducational assessment of preschool children (4th ed., pp. 137-153). Mahwah, NJ: Erlbaum.

Bracken, B. A., Keith, L. K., & Walker, K. C. (1998). Assessment of preschool behavior and social-emotional functioning: A review of thirteen third-party instruments. *Assessment in Rehabilitation and Exceptionality, 1*, 331-346.

Bradley-Johnson, S. (2001). Cognitive assessment for the youngest of children: A critical review of tests. *Journal of Psychoeducational Assessment, 19*, 19-44.

D'Angiulli, A., & Sullivan, R. (2010). Early specialized foster care, developmental outcomes and home salivary cortisol patterns in prenatally substance-exposed infants. *Children and Youth Services Review, 32*, 460-465.

Evans, L. D., & Bradley-Jonson, S. (1988). A review of recently developed measures of adaptive behavior. *Psychology in the Schools, 25*, 276-287.

Flanagan, D. P., & Alfonso, V. C. (1995). A critical review of the technical characteristics of new and recently revised intelligence tests for preschool children. *Journal of Psychoeducational Assessment, 13*, 66-90.

Folio, M. R., & Fewell R. R. (2000). *Peabody Developmental Motor Scales* (2nd ed.). Austin, TX: PRO-ED.

Frankenburg, W. K., Dodds, J. B., Archer, P., Bresnick, B., Maschka, P., Edelman, N., et al. (1992). *Denver Developmental Screening Test-II (DDST-II).* Denver, CO: Denver Developmental Materials, Inc.

Kaufman, A. S., Flanagan, D. P., Alfonso, V. C., & Mascolo, J. T. (2006). Review of Wechsler Intelligence Scale for Children, Fourth Edition (WISC-IV). *Journal of Psychoeducational Assessment, 24*, 278-295.

Mardell-Czudnowski, C., & Goldenberg, D. S. (1998). *Developmental Indicators for the Assessment of Learning-Third Edition (DIAL-3).* Circle Pines, MN: AGS.

Matson, J. L., Mahan, S., Hess, J. A., & Fodstad, J. C. (2010). Effect of developmental quotient on symptoms of inattention and impulsivity among toddlers with Autism Spectrum Disorders. *Research in Developmental Disabilities, 31*, 464-469.

McGrew, K. S., & Flanagan, D. P. (1998). *The intelligence test desk reference (ITDR): Gf-Gc cross-battery assessment.* Boston, MA: Allyn & Bacon.

Newborg, J. (2005a). *Battelle Developmental Inventory, 2nd Edition.* Itasca, IL: Riverside Publishing.

Newborg, J. (2005b). *Battelle Developmental Inventory, 2nd Edition, Examiner's manual.* Itasca, IL: Riverside Publishing.

Newborg, J., Stock, J. R., Wnek, L., Guidubaldi, J., & Svinicki, J. (1984). *Battelle Developmental Inventory, Examiner's Manual.* Allen, TX: DLM Teaching Resources.

Oades-Sese, G., & Alfonso, V. C. (2003, August). *A critical review of the psychometric integrity of preschool language tests.* Poster presented at the annual meeting of the American Psychological Association, Toronto, Ontario, Canada.

Oades-Sese, G., & Alfonso, V. C. (2008). *A critical review of the psychometric integrity of preschool language tests*. Manuscript in preparation.

Sparrow, S. S., Balla, D. A., & Cicchetti, D. V. (1998). *Vineland Social-Emotional Early Childhood Scales*. Circle Pines, MN: AGS.

Wagner, R. K., Torgesen, J. K., & Rashotte, C. A. (1999). *Comprehensive Test of Phonological Processing*. Austin, TX: PRO-ED.

Wechsler, D. (2002). *Wechsler Preschool and Primary Scale of Intelligence-Third Edition (WPPSI-III)*. San Antonio, TX: Psychological Corporation.

Woodcock, R. W., McGrew, K. S., & Mather, N. (2001). *Woodcock-Johnson III Tests of Achievement*. Itasca, IL: Riverside Publishing.

Zimmerman, I. L., Steiner, V. G., & Pond, R. E. (2002). *Preschool Language Scale, Fourth Edition*. San Antonio, TX: Psychological Corporation.

Understanding Parent Reports of Children's Attention Behaviors:
Role of Children's Attention Skills, Temperament, and Home Environment

Danielle D. Brown
Howard University

Tara N. Weatherholt & Barbara M. Burns
University of Louisville

This study aimed to investigate factors that influence the assessment of child attention behaviors by parents from low-income households. This study extends previous research on attention by investigating child and environmental factors as predictors of parent reports of attention behaviors. Questionnaires from 123 parents from low-income households concerning child attention behaviors, child temperament, and home environment were completed. Child attention skills were assessed using three computerized attention network tasks. The hypothesis that child attention skills, child temperament, and the home environment would be additive in its predictive relation to parent reports of problem attention behaviors was supported. Specifically, higher ratings of problem attention behavior were predicted by lower executive attention skills, lower effortful control, higher surgency/extraversion and negative affect, and higher home chaos. The results have implications for intervention development, research on parent reports, and the diagnoses of attention problems.

Child attention problems are typically assessed using parent reports of attention on behavioral rating scales (Diamond & Squires, 1993; Sax & Kautz, 2003; Tripp, Schaughency, & Bronwyn, 2006). Previous research has found parent reports of attention behaviors to be weakly related to other measures of attention (Brewis, 2002; Davis, Burns, Snyder, & Robinson, 2007; Gimpel & Kuhn, 2000; Mitchell & Quittner, 1996; Mitsis, McKay, Schultz, Newcorn, & Halperin, 2000; Pelham, Fabiano, & Massetti, 2005; Power et al., 1998; Tripp et al., 2006). More

All correspondence should be addressed to Danielle D. Brown, Ph.D., Department of Psychology, Howard University, 525 Bryant St., NW, Washington, DC 20059. Electronic mail may be sent to: danielle.brown@howard.edu.

research is needed to examine factors associated with parents' ratings of attention behaviors. In the current study, we examined cognitive measures of attention skills as well as measures of temperament and the home environment as factors predicting parent reports.

A better understanding of parent report of attention behaviors may be particularly important for families from low-income families. First, children from low-income families may be at risk for developing attention problems. In a nationally representative sample of 300 children, Froehlich et al. (2007) found that children from low-income families were more likely to fulfill criteria for Attention-Deficit/Hyperactivity Disorder (ADHD) than children from higher-income families. Children from low-income families are also more likely to be diagnosed with an attention disorder (Diamond & Squires, 1993; Döpnfer et al., 2008; Schneider & Eisenberg, 2006). Despite this pattern, few studies have directly examined parent reports of attention behaviors in children living in low-income families. The current study addresses this issue by characterizing factors that underlie parent reports of attention behaviors in children from low-income families.

Predicting Parent Reports of Attention Behaviors

Previous studies have addressed the question as to what underlies parent reports of attention problems in three ways. First, some studies have examined cognitive measures of attention as predictors (Brewis, 2002; Brown & Whynn, 1982; Mitchell & Quittner, 1996). The current study used computerized attention tasks developed by Berger and colleagues (Berger, Jones, Rothbart, & Posner, 2000) as cognitive measures of attention. The tasks measure independent skills associated with the orienting, alerting, and executive attention networks (Fan, McCandliss, Sommer, Raz, & Posner, 2002; Fernandez-Dugue & Posner, 2001; Posner & Petersen, 1990). The orienting network accounts for shifts in attention; the alerting network accounts for the ability to achieve and maintain a vigilant state; and the executive network manages goal directed behavior, target detection, conflict resolution, task switching, the inhibition of automatic responses, and the allocation of attentional resources. The attention network tasks allow for the assessment of individual differences in attention skills and have previously been used to measure attention in children from low-income families (Chang & Burns, 2005; Mezzacappa, 2004; Weatherholt, Harris, Burns, & Clement, 2006).

A second predictor that has been hypothesized to underlie parent reports is child temperament. Rothbart and colleagues define temperament as patterns of reactivity that are biologically based and stable and can be measured on three dimensions: effortful control, surgency/extraversion, and negative affect (Rothbart, Ahadi, Hershey, & Fisher, 2001). Temperament dimensions have been shown to be closely related to attention behaviors. Effortful control includes mechanisms of inhibition and the allocation of attention (Olson, Sameroff, Kerr,

Lopez, & Wellman, 2005; Rothbart, Ellis, Rueda, & Posner, 2003; Rothbart, Sheese, & Posner, 2007); extraversion incorporates mechanisms of impulsivity (Davis, Bruce, & Gunnar, 2002) and high activity (Rothbart et al., 2007); and negative affect may include reactive components that motivate problem behaviors in negative social interactions (Eisenberg et al., 2005; Olson et al., 2005). Previous research has shown associations between attention deficit disorder and low effortful control (Willcutt, Doyle, Nigg, Faraone, & Pennington, 2005) and links between parent reports of attention behaviors and child temperament (Davis et al., 2002; Murray & Kochanska, 2002; Olson et al., 2005).

A third factor underlying parent assessments of attention problems centers on the home environment. The degree of chaos in the home, which includes levels of noise, unstructured stimulation, and unpredictability, has been shown to predict parent reports of attention behaviors (Dilworth-Bart, Khurshid, & Vandell, 2007). Home chaos has been shown to relate to attention problems (Evans, Gonnella, Marcynyszyn, Gentile, & Salpekar, 2005; NICHD Early Child Care Research Network, 2003; Wachs, 1979) and to parent reports of attention behaviors (Dumas et al., 2005). One study found that chaos predicted parent ratings of child behavior over what was predicted by parenting variables (e.g., maternal warmth and hostility; Coldwell, Pike, & Dunn, 2006). Other studies have suggested that parent reports are more accurate for child behaviors that occur within the home (Mitsis et al., 2000; Sayal & Taylor, 2005), but show little agreement with teacher reports of child behavior that occur in school (Brewis, 2002; de Nijs et al., 2004). Some researchers suggest that home chaos may contribute to parent reports of children's attention behavior through its effect on child behavior. For example, children who live in homes with high chaos may display attentive behavior problems at home, but not display such problems in a less chaotic school environment. In addition, children from low-income families are more likely to live in low quality households (Dilworth-Bart et al., 2007), particularly homes with a higher level of chaos (Dumas et al., 2005; Evans, 2004; Evans et al., 2005; Matheny, Wachs, Ludwig, & Phillips, 1995).

Current Study

There is a need for a more comprehensive understanding of the underlying basis of parent reports of attention problems. Previous research has investigated how cognitive aspects of attention, temperament, and aspects of the home environment independently contribute to parent reports. Such a comprehensive understanding is of special significance for populations shown to be at risk for developing attention problems. The current study examines multiple predictors of parent reports of attention behaviors in children from low-income families. Cognitive measures of children's attention skills as well as child temperament and home chaos were investigated as predictors of parent reports. It is hypothesized that each factor will be additive in its predictive relation. We expect that better performance on the attention network tasks, higher ratings on the temperament dimension of effortful control and lower ratings on the surgency/extraversion and negative affect dimensions, and lower home chaos will relate to lower parent ratings of problem attention behaviors. The current study contributes to the literature by providing the first examination of the role of multiple predictors of reports made by parents from low-income families.

Method

Participants. One hundred twenty-three children (56 boys, 67 girls) between 48- and 91-months-old ($M = 67.20$, $SD = 11.50$) and their primary caregivers from low-income families were recruited from Head Start programs and a local public health clinic. Most (98%) of the primary caregivers were mothers. In terms of maternal education, 24% did not have a high school diploma, 28% had a high school diploma or GED, and 48% had some education beyond high school. The sample consisted of 88% African American and 10% European American children; 2% of the children were classified as "other" in the category of race/ethnicity. Mothers reported that their children had not been diagnosed with attention disorders and they did not take medications that would alter cognitive performance.

Measures. *Parent reports of attention behaviors.* Mothers rated child behavior on 26 items of the *Conner's Parent Rating Scale-Revised* (CPRS-R) that cluster into two scales, an ADHD index and a *Diagnostic and Statistical Manual of Mental Disorders, Fourth Edition* (DSM-IV; APA, 1994) scale (Conners, 2000; Conners, Sitarenios, Parker, & Epstein, 1998). The ADHD index includes items designed to distinguish children with an attention deficit disorder from children without an attention deficit disorder. The DSM-IV scale includes items that directly relate to the criteria described in the DSM-IV. The T-scores for the ADHD index and DSM-IV scale were used as dependent variables in the current study. Possible scores ranged from 38 to 90 ($M = 50$, $SD = 10$). Conners (2000) has reported internal reliability that ranged from .89 to .95 (Cronbach's *alpha*) and test-retest reliability (correlation over an 8-week interval) of .72 for the ADHD index and .76 for the DSM-IV scale. Convergent reliability as measured by the correlation between parent and teacher reports ranged from .44 to .49. Both the ADHD index and the DSM-IV scale were found to discriminate children diagnosed with attention deficit disorders from children without diagnoses.

Child attention skills. Three computerized tasks measured each of the three attention networks identified by Posner and Peterson (1990; see Berger et al., 2000 and Chang & Burns, 2005 for additional details regarding tasks). A touch screen monitor was placed on a table in front of the child. Children were instructed to touch the stimulus on the monitor when it appeared and all responses were recorded. Each task consisted of 32 trials and up to 3 sets of practice trials. Performance was measured by accuracy and median reaction time (MRT) for correct trials. Possible MRTs ranged from a minimum of 500 ms for all attention network tasks to a maximum of 5000 ms for the orienting and executive tasks and a maximum of 3000 ms for the alerting task. Mean accuracy and MRT for each of the three tasks are shown in Table 1. As is typical in attention research with children, MRT best captured individual differences in performance on the attention network tasks. MRT for correct trials were used as predictor variables in subsequent analyses.

The orienting task measures spatial orientation of attention. The child is presented with two fish bowls to the left and right of a fixation point. A trial consists of a fixation stimulus, followed by a cue, and then the fish. The cue appears on each bowl with equal probability and is defined by a color change in one of the fish bowls. The cue and fish can appear in either the same fish bowl or opposite fish bowls. The alerting task measures changes in vigilance following presentations of warning signals. An animal appears on the screen for each trial. An auditory warning signal is presented in half of the trials and at different intervals. The executive task measures one aspect of executive attention, the ability to resolve a conflict. Two houses with a picture in each are presented at the left and right bottom of the screen. A stimulus appears at the top of the screen. The child is instructed to touch the house with the identical picture as fast as possible.

Two studies have examined reliability of the attention network tasks with variable findings. Test-retest reliability correlations ranged from .52 to .87 for adults that were administered the tasks within the same session (Fan et al., 2002); no significant correlations were found over 6.5 months for children (Reuda et al., 2004). Split-half reliability correlations ranged from .37 to .94; a correlation of

Table 1

Means and Standard Deviations for Performance on Attention Network Tasks, Temperament, and Home Chaos

Variables	Mean	Standard Deviation
Orienting task accuracy	.99	.02
Alerting task accuracy	.99	.03
Executive task accuracy MRT	.95	.09
Orienting task MRT	1066.60	196.77
Alerting task MRT	894.08	167.75
Executive task MRT	1649.26	417.31
Effortful Control	5.22	0.66
Surgency/Extraversion	5.22	0.66
Negative Affect	5.52	1.12
Home Chaos	19.41	3.56

.02 was found for the orienting task. Concurrent validity has been examined for an adult version of the tasks as well (Weaver, Bédarda, McAuliffe, & Parkkari, 2009). Performance on the attention network task explained 69% of the variance in performance on the Useful Field of View, which assesses processing speed, divided attention, and selective attention. In terms of discriminate validity, adults with high working memory capacity significantly outperformed those with low working memory capacity on the executive network task (Redick & Engle, 2006).

Child temperament. A parent-report measure was used to examine child temperament. The *Children's Behavior Questionnaire (Short Form Version 1; CBQ)* was designed to assess 3- to 7-year old children's effortful control, surgency/extraversion, and negative affect (Rothbart et al., 2001). Effortful control consists of attentional focusing, inhibitory control, low intensity pleasure, and perceptual sensitivity scales. Surgency/extraversion consists of impulsivity, high intensity pleasure, activity level, and shyness scales. Negative affect consists of discomfort, fear, anger/frustration, sadness, and soothability scales. Mothers rated the 98 items based on a 7-point Likert scale with 1 being "extremely untrue" for the child and 7 being "extremely true" for the child. Possible ratings ranged from 1 to 7 for all scales and factors. Mean ratings for the three factors are shown in Table 1. Rothbart et al. (2001) report an internal consistency reliability of .73 to .75 across all scales. Convergent validity based on parent agreement correlations was .37 and .41 across all scales.

Home environment. Mothers were asked to complete the *Confusion, Hubbub, and Order Scale* (CHAOS; Matheny et al., 1995), a 15-item questionnaire concerning the amount of environmental confusion in the home. Some of the items are "There is very little commotion in our home," "You can't hear yourself think in our home," and "No matter what our family plans, it usually doesn't seem to work out." The items were presented in a True/False format with approximately half of the items reversed. Possible CHAOS scores ranged from 15 to 30 and the mean scores are reported in Table 1. Matheny et al. (1995) report an internal consistency of .79 (coefficient *alpha*) and a test-retest reliability of .74 (correlation over a 12-month interval). Interrater reliability yielded a correlation of .77 on a version of the CHAOS that included a Likert scale (Hart, Petrill, Deckard, & Thompson, 2007). Sufficient validity was also observed when the CHAOS was compared to an observational measure of the home environment (Matheny et al., 1995).

Cognitive ability. The *Kaufman Brief-Intelligence Test* (KBIT; Kaufman & Kaufman, 1990), a standardized cognitive ability test with vocabulary and matrices subtests, was used. On the vocabulary subtest, the participant was asked to name various pictures. The matrices subtest is a measure of analogical reasoning in which participants must complete a visual analogy. Standard scores for overall cognitive ability were used. Possible scores ranged from 40 to 160 ($M = 100$, $SD = 15$). Children's scores had a mean of 89.81 ($SD = 10.65$). Internal (split-half) reliability ranged from .89 to .92 and test-retest reliability (over a mean of 21 days) of .92 (Kaufman & Kaufman, 1990). Concurrent validity that compared the KBIT with other measures of cognitive ability ranged from .23 to .76.

Procedure. All procedures and methods were approved by the university's institutional review board. Mothers provided written informed consent for their children and themselves. Children provided oral assent prior to participating in the study. The children and their mothers were informed that they could withdraw their participation at any point during the study. All children completed the three computerized attention network tasks followed by the cognitive ability assessment while mothers completed the questionnaires in a separate room. Questionnaires were administered in a standard order for all participants. A research assistant read all items from the questionnaires to the mothers.

Results

Maternal reports of their children's attention behaviors, as indicated by ratings on the CPRS scales, are described first and depicted in Figure 1. According to Conners (2000), below average (scores below 45) and average (scores ranging from 45 to 55) scores are not considered problematic while above average scores (above 55) indicate attention problems. On average, parents indicated attention problems on the ADHD index ($M = 56.39$, $SD = 12.35$) and on the DSM-IV scale ($M = 58.72$, $SD = 12.64$) in their children. As shown in Figure 1, approximately half of the mothers reported attention problems in their children.

Predictors of Parent Reports of Attention Behaviors. Means for all predictor variables are shown in Table 1. Preliminary correlational analyses were performed to determine whether children's chronological age, gender, and cognitive ability were related to any of the variables of interest. Chronological age was significantly correlated with orienting MRT ($r = -.43$, $p < .001$), alerting MRT ($r = -.41$, $p < .001$), and executive MRT ($r = -.43$, $p < .001$). Gender was significantly correlated with surgency/extraversion ($r = -.28$, $p < .01$). Cognitive ability was significantly correlated with ratings on the ADHD index ($r = -.20$, $p < .01$) and effortful control ($r = .19$, $p < .01$). Thus, all three variables were statistically controlled in subsequent analyses.

The data were submitted to correlational and multiple regression analyses in order to test the hypothesis that children's attention skills, temperament, and home environments each predicted parent reports of attention behaviors. Results for correlational analyses are reported in Table 2. In the regression analysis, chronological age, gender, and cognitive ability were controlled and entered in step 1. MRTs for the three attention network tasks were added as predictor variables in step 2; mothers' ratings of effortful control, surgency/extraversion, and negative affect in step 3; and ratings of home chaos in step 4. The overall regression model was significant for ratings on the CPRS, $F(10,112) = 10.48$, $p < .001$ (see Table 3). Only the results for the ADHD index are reported given

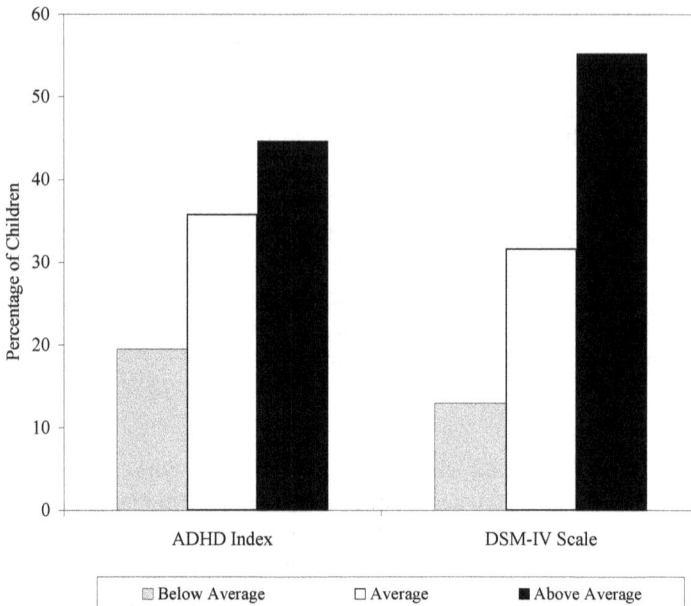

Figure 1. Percentage of children categorized on the ADHD Index and DSM-IV Scale of the CPRS as below average, average, and above average. Categorizations are based on T-scores and the guidelines in Connors (2000).

the high correlation between the ADHD index and the DSM-IV scale ($r = .90$, $p < .001$). Findings for each predictor variable are discussed separately.

Attention skills. Mothers' ratings on the CPRS were positively correlated with MRT on the executive task (see Table 2). Performance on the orienting and alerting tasks was not significantly correlated to parent reports of attention problems. Regression analyses produced similar results. After considering the effects of chronological age, gender, and cognitive ability, performance on the attention networks tasks accounted for 11% of the variance. Only executive MRT was significant (see Table 3). Children who rated higher in attention problems had slower responses on the executive attention task.

Child temperament. Mothers' ratings of attention problems were negatively correlated with effortful control and positively correlated with surgency/ extraversion and negative affect (see Table 2). The addition of temperament significantly contributed to the regression model. The regression coefficient for effortful control was significant and negative (see Table 3). Children who rated lower in effortful control had higher attention behavior ratings. The coefficients for surgency/extraversion and negative affect were significant and positive. Higher ratings of attention problems were predicted by higher ratings in the latter two temperament aspects.

Table 2

Correlations of Parent Reports of Attention Problems, Performance on Attention Network Tasks, Temperament, and Home Chaos Controlling for Chronological Age, Gender, and Cognitive Ability

Variables	1	2	3	4	5	6	7	8
1. ADHD Index	---							
2. Orienting MRT	.03	---						
3. Alerting MRT	.08	.53**	---					
4. Executive MRT	.33**	.35**	.33**	---				
5. Effortful Control	-.44**	-.07	.05	-.20*	---			
6. Surgency/ Extraversion	.29*	-.01	.07	.04	-.18	---		
7. Negative Affect	.39**	-.01	.10	.21*	-.12	-.00	---	
8. Home Chaos	.37**	.03	.16	.11	-.27**	.05	-.17	---

$*p < .05$ $**p < .01$

Home chaos. Mothers' ratings of home chaos were positively correlated with reports of attention problem behaviors (see Table 2). Home chaos significantly contributed to the regression model, accounting for 4% of the variance. Children who lived in homes characterized by higher amounts of home chaos had higher attention problem behavior ratings.

Overall, the results support the hypothesis that parent reports of attention behaviors are predicted by multiple factors in an additive way. Each factor explained additional variance in parent reports of attention problems.

Discussion

The current study characterized parent reports of attention behaviors of children from low-income families. Approximately half of the children were rated as having attention problems. This is consistent with research showing higher rates of attention problems in low-income populations (Breznitz & Norman, 1998; Mezzacappa, 2004; Norman & Breznitz, 1992; Schneider & Eisenberg, 2006). Other studies, however, suggest that parents overestimate attention behavior problems (Gimpel & Kuhn, 2000). The current results indicate that in addition to cognitive attention skills, other factors underlie parent ratings of children's attention behaviors.

Attention Skills

The current findings show that parent reports of attention behaviors were predicted by individual differences in children's executive attention. Increases in ratings of attention problems were predicted by decreases in executive attention.

This suggests that children's actual attention skills relate to how parents rate their children's attention behaviors. However, executive attention only accounted for 11% of the individual differences in parent reports. This finding is problematic because parent report measures are designed to assess attention disorders (Conners et al., 1998; Mahone, 2005), which have deficits primarily in the executive attention network (Konrad, Neufang, Hanisch, Fink, & Hepertz-Dahlmann, 2006; Max et al., 2005; Willcutt et al., 2005). Research has previously found an association between actual attention disorders and executive attention (Johnson et al., 2008). Thus, we expected a larger relation between parent reports of problem attention behaviors and cognitive measures of executive attention skills. Weak relations have previously been found (Brewis, 2002; Davis et al., 2007; Gimpel & Kuhn, 2000; Mitchell & Quittner, 1996; Mitsis et al., 2000; Pelham et al., 2005; Power et al., 1998; Tripp et al., 2006). It is unclear whether this weak relation between attention disorders and executive attention skills is due to parent perceptions of children's attention skills or differences in behavioral and cognitive measures of attention. This remains controversial. Swanson and colleagues (2004) suggest that cognitive measures of attention may not be sensitive or specific to attention disorders.

Temperament

Child temperament predicted a substantial amount of variation in parent reports of child attention behaviors. Children low in effortful control and high

Table 3

Summary of Hierarchical Regression Analysis for Attention Network Tasks Performance, Temperament, and Home Chaos Predicting Parent Ratings on the CPRS-R

	Variable	ΔR^2	B	β
1.	Chronological Age		0.17	.16
	Gender		-1.16	-.05
	Cognitive Ability	0.07*	-0.25	-.22*
2.	Orienting MRT		-0.01	-.11
	Alerting MRT		0.00	.01
	Executive MRT	0.11**	0.01	.40**
3.	Effortful Control		-6.29	-.33**
	Surgency/Extraversion		3.56	.23**
	Negative Affect	0.26**	4.28	.30**
4.	Home Chaos	0.04**	0.77	.22**

*p < .05   **p <.01

in surgency/extraversion and negative affect were rated as higher in attention problem behaviors. This supports previous research connecting child temperament to attention development (Nigg, Goldsmith, & Sachek, 2004; Rothbart, Ahadi et al., 2001; Rothbart et al., 2003; Rothbart et al., 2007), attention disorders (Foley, McClowry, & Castellanos, 2008; Willcutt et al., 2005), and parent reports of attention behavior (Davis et al., 2002; Murray & Kochanska, 2002; Olson et al., 2005).

While research shows that temperament impacts attention development, the two are theoretically distinct (Chang & Burns, 2005; Derryberry & Rothbart, 1997; Rothbart et al., 2003). Specifically, effortful control regulates emotional and cognitive aspects of temperament. However, low effortful control has been shown to be a marker for attention problems (Foley et al., 2008; Willcutt et al., 2005) because it requires attention skills such as inhibition and attentional focusing. Parents do not appear to distinguish behavior associated with attention problems from behavior resulting from other aspects of temperament. Children high in surgency/extraversion exhibit high activity, which may resemble attention problems. Children high in negative affect exhibit low soothability, which may also resemble attention problems. For example, a child who cannot be easily soothed after a period of excitement may appear to be disorganized which is similar to behaviors associated with attention problems.

Home Environment

We found that parents who rated their homes as higher in chaos also rated their children higher in attention behavior problems. Previous research has shown a relation between home chaos and attention skills (Coldwell et al., 2006; Dumas et al., 2005; NICHD Early Child Care Research Network, 2003; Wachs, 1979); however, there was not a significant relation between home chaos and cognitive measures of attention in the current study. Taken together, these two findings lend support for context-related variability in child behavior (Brewis, 2002; Murray et al., 2007; Pelham et al., 2005). Children who live in highly chaotic homes may exhibit attention behavior problems at home, but not in more structured or predictable environments (e.g., school settings) and may not have cognitive deficits in attention. This context-related variability is supported by research showing that, although parents are accurate at rating child behaviors that occur within the home (Mitsis et al., 2000; Sayal & Taylor, 2005), they show little agreement with teachers across home and school contexts (de Nijs et al., 2004). Child behavior in school contexts may be a better predictor of attention deficits given that the amount of chaos may vary less between classrooms than between homes and that previous research has shown that teacher reports are more accurate than parent reports (Power et al., 1998; Tripp et al., 2006).

Study Limitations

The use of parent ratings of child temperament and the home environment rather than observational measures may limit the current findings. It is possible that similarities in the method of assessment account for the relation to reports of attention behaviors. The findings, however, are consistent with previous studies that have employed observational measures of temperament (Murray & Kochanska, 2002; Nigg et al., 2004; Olson et al., 2005). Parent ratings of child temperament, child attention behaviors, and the home environment may also be related through parent factors (e.g., parenting stress, temperament, and maternal sensitivity and warmth) that were not measured in the current study. For example, aspects of high levels of home chaos and parenting stress have been shown to negatively impact aspects of the parenting-child relationship that are associated with child outcomes (Evans, Maxwell, & Hart, 1999; McKay & Pickens, 1996; Magill-Evans & Harrison, 2001). Thus, parental factors may be an important contributor to parents' perception of children's attention behaviors.

Another limitation of the current findings is the limited evidence of reliability and validity on child versions of the attention network tasks. The low reliability across 6.5 months for specific components of the child tasks may relate to developmental changes (Reuda et al., 2004); however, researchers need to examine this further. There are very few studies demonstrating the validity of the attention network task for children. One study found evidence of discriminate validity in that children diagnosed with ADHD had slower responses on executive attention tasks (Konrad et al., 2006).

Implications for Research and Practice

There are several important implications that follow from the current study. Previous research has often examined parent reports of attention behaviors in relation to teacher reports, cognitive measures of attention, and/or diagnoses of attention disorders. The resulting conclusions from these studies were that parent reports are largely inaccurate predictors of children's attention problems. Although researchers have proposed reasons for these inaccuracies based on their findings, few studies have empirically addressed this in a comprehensive manner. Considering that parent suggestions and reports are important in diagnosing attention deficits (Sax & Kautz, 2003), it is critical to better understand the basis for parent reports of children's attention problems. Given the similar importance of teacher suggestions and reports of attention deficits (Sax & Kautz), it is also critical to understand the predictors of teacher reports of attention behaviors.

Second, our findings have clear implications for the diagnoses of attention deficit disorders. We found that while parent reports were partly based on children's actual attention skills, they also varied according to home and other child characteristics. Practitioners' reliance on such measures suggests that diagnoses also vary according to similar factors. Similarly, Schneider and Eisenberg (2006) found that the probability that a child received an attention deficit diagnosis varied according to child, family, geographic, and school characteristics. Such characteristics were seemingly unrelated to actual attention skills, but had an impact on an ADHD diagnosis.

In addition, the current study combined with the findings of Schneider and Eisenberg (2006) also imply the need for further examination of the predictors of both reports of attention behaviors and attention deficit diagnoses. Structural equation modeling (SEM) is a powerful statistical method that has several advantages for the examination of reports of attention behaviors. One relevant advantage is the ability to test relations among predictor variables, outcome variables, and predictor and outcome variables (Hoyle, 1995). For example, SEM can examine the role of parent characteristics in parent ratings of child temperament, child attention behaviors, and the home environment. The relation between parent reports and attention deficit diagnoses as outcome variables can also be examined within the same structural model.

Finally, future research should focus on interventions that educate parents on optimal home environments for children's attention development. These interventions can target parents who rate their children as high in attention behavior problems, but whose children do not receive a formal diagnosis. The results of this study suggest that optimal home environments may include reducing home chaos and increasing the fit between child temperament and the home environment. In cases of diagnosis, clinicians should consider including assessments of the home environment as well as child temperament in their battery of parent reports of attention problems. Evidence of the predictive power and accuracy of parent assessments of attention behaviors, although mixed, has received little consideration. Given its central role in diagnoses, it is important to understand individual differences in parent assessments.

References

American Psychiatric Association. (1994*). Diagnostic and statistical manual of mental disorders* (4th ed.). Washington, DC: Author.

Berger, A., Jones, L., Rothbart, M. K., & Posner, M. I. (2000). Computerized games to study the development of attention in childhood. *Behavior Research Methods, Instruments, & Computers, 32*(2), 297-303.

Brewis, A. (2002). Social and biological measures of hyperactivity and inattention: Are they describing similar underlying constructs of child behavior? *Social Biology, 49*(1/2), 99-115.

Breznitz, Z., & Norman, G. (1998). Differences in concentration ability among low- and high-SES Israeli students: A follow-up study. *The Journal of Genetic Psychology, 159*(1), 82-93.

Brown, R. T., & Wynne, M. E. (1982). Correlates of teacher ratings, sustained attention, and impulsivity in hyperactive and normal boys. *Journal of Clinical Child Psychology, 11*(3), 242-267.

Chang, F., & Burns, B. M. (2005). Attention in preschoolers: Associations with effortful control and motivation. *Child Development, 76*(1), 247-263.

Coldwell, J., Pike, A., & Dunn, J. (2006). Household chaos – links with parenting and child behaviour. *Journal of Child Psychology and Psychiatry, 47*(11), 1116-1122.

Conners, C. K. (2000). *Conners' Rating Scales-Revised: Instruments for Use with Children and Adolescents.* Tonawanda, New York: Multi-Health Systems.

Conners, C. K., Sitarenios, G., Parker, J. D. A., & Epstein, J. N. (1998). The revised Conners' Parent Rating Scale (CPRS-R): Factor structure, reliability, and criterion validity. *Journal of Abnormal Child Psychology, 26*(4), 257-268.

Davis, D. W., Burns, B., Snyder, E., & Robinson, J. (2007). Attention problems in very low birth weight preschoolers: Are new screening measures needed for this special population? *Journal of Child and Adolescent Psychiatric Nursing, 20*(2), 74-85.

Davis, E. P., Bruce, J., & Gunnar, M. R. (2002). The anterior attention network: Associations with temperament and neuroendocrine activity in 6-year-old children. *Developmental Psychobiology, 40*, 43-56.

de Nijs, P. F. A., Ferdinand, R. F., de Bruin, E. I., Dekker, M. C. J., van Duijn, C. M., & Verhulst, F. C. (2004). Attention-deficit/hyperactivity disorder (ADHD): Parents' judgment about school, teachers' judgment about home. *European Child and Adolescent Psychiatry, 13*, 315-320.

Derryberry, D., & Rothbart, M. K. (1997). Reactive and effortful processes in the organization of temperament. *Development and Psychopathology, 9*, 633-652.

Diamond, K. E., & Squires, J. (1993). The role of parental report in the screening and assessment of young children. *Journal of Early Intervention, 17*(2), 107-115.

Dilworth-Bart, J. E., Khurshid, A., & Vandell, D. L. (2007). Do maternal stress and home environment mediate the relation between early income-to-need and 54-months attentional abilities? *Infant and Child Development, 16*(5), 525-552.

Döpfner, M. F., Breuer, D., Wille, N., Erhart, M., Ravens-Sieberer, U., & the BELLA study group (2008). How often do children meet ICD-10/DSM-IV criteria of attention deficit-/hyperactivity disorder and hyperkinetic disorder? Parent-based prevalence rates in a national sample – results of the BELLA study. *European Child and Adolescent Psychiatry, 17*(supplement 1), 59-70.

Dumas, J. E., Nissley, J., Nordstrom, A., Smith, E. P., Prinz, R. J., & Levine D. W. (2005). Home chaos: Sociodemographic, parenting, interactional, and child correlates. *Journal of Clinical Child and Adolescent Psychology, 34*(1), 93-104.

Eisenberg, N., Sadovsky, A., Spinrad, T. L., Fabes, R. A., Losoya, S. H., Valient, C., et al. (2005). The relations of problem behavior status to children's negative emotionality, effortful control, and impulsivity: Concurrent relations and prediction of change. *Developmental Psychology, 41*(1), 193-211.

Evans, G. W. (2004). The environment of childhood poverty. *American Psychologist, 59*(2), 77-92.

Evans, G. W., Gonnella, C., Marcynyszyn, L. A., Gentile, L., & Salpekar, N. (2005). The role of chaos in poverty and children's socioemotional adjustment. *Psychological Science, 16*(7), 560-565.

Evans, G. W., Maxwell, L. E., & Hart, B. (1999). Parental language and verbal responsiveness to children in crowded homes. *Developmental Psychology, 35*(4), 1020-1023.

Fan, J., McCandliss, B. D., Sommer, T., Raz, A., & Posner, M. I. (2002). Testing the efficiency and independence of attentional networks. *Journal of Cognitive Neurosciences, 14*(3), 340-347.

Fernandez-Dugue, D., & Posner, M. I. (2001). Brain imaging of attentional networks in normal and pathological states. *Journal of Clinical and Experimental Neuropsychology, 23*(1), 74-93.

Foley, M., McClowry, S. G., & Castellanos, F. X. (2008). The relationship between attention deficit hyperactivity disorder and child temperament. *Journal of Applied Developmental Psychology 29*, 157–169.

Froehlich, T. E., Lanphear, B. P., Epstein, J. N., Barbaresi, W. J., Katusic, S. K., & Kahn, R. S. (2007). Prevalence, recognition, and treatment of attention-deficit/hyperactivity disorder in a National Sample of US Children. *Archives of Pediatrics & Adolescent Medicine, 161*(9), 857-864.

Gimpel, G. A., & Kuhn, B. R. (2000). Maternal report of attention deficit hyperactivity disorder symptoms in preschool children. *Child: Care, Health and Development, 26*(3), 163-179.

Hart, S. A., Petrill, S. A., Deckard, K. D., & Thompson, L. A. (2007). SES and CHAOS as environmental mediators of cognitive ability: A longitudinal genetic analysis. *Intelligence, 35*, 233-242.

Hoyle, R. H. (1995). The structural equation modeling approach: Basic concepts and fundamental issues. In R. H. Hoyle (Ed.), *Structural equation modeling: Concepts, issues and applications* (pp. 1-15). Thousand Oaks, CA: Sage.

Johnson, K. A., Robertson, I. H., Barry, E., Mulligan, A., Da´ibhis, A., Daly, M., et al. (2008). Impaired conflict resolution and alerting in children with ADHD: Evidence from the Attention Network Task (ANT). *Journal of Child Psychology and Psychiatry, 49*(12), 1339-1347.

Kaufman, A. S., & Kaufman, N. L. (1990). *Kaufman Brief Intelligence Test.* Circle Pine, MN: American Guidance Service.

Konrad, K., Neufang, S., Hanisch, C., Fink, G. R., & Herpertz-Dahlmann, B. (2006). Dysfunctional attentional networks in children with attention deficit/hyperactivity disorder: Evidence from an event-related functional magnetic resonance imaging study. *Biological Psychiatry, 59*, 643-651.

Magill-Evans, J., & Harrison, M. J. (2001). Parent–child interactions, parenting stress, and developmental outcomes at 4 years. *Children's Health Care, 30*(2), 135–150.

Mahone, E. M. (2005). Measurement of attention and related functions in the preschool child. *Mental Retardation and Developmental Disabilities, 11*, 216-225.

Matheny, A. P., Wachs, T. D., Ludwig, J. L., & Phillips, K. (1995). Bringing order out of chaos: Psychometric characteristics of the confusion, hubbub, and order scale. *Journal of Applied Developmental Psychology, 16*, 429-444.

Max, J. E., Manes, F. F., Robertson, B. A. M., Mathews, K., Fox, P. T., & Lancaster, J. (2005). Prefrontal and executive attention network lesions and the development of attention-deficit/hyperactivity symptomatology. *Journal of the American Academy of Child and Adolescent Psychiatry, 44*(5), 443-450.

Mezzacappa, E. (2004). Alerting, orienting, and executive attention: Developmental properties and sociodemographic correlates in an epidemiological sample of young, urban children. *Child Development, 75*(5), 1373-1386.

McKay, J. M., & Pickens, J. (1996). Inventoried and observed stress in parent-child interactions. *Current Psychology, 15*(3), 223-234.

Mitchell, T. V., & Quittner, A. L. (1996). Multimethod study of attention and behavior problems in hearing-impaired children. *Journal of Clinical Child Psychology, 25*(1), 83-96.

Mitsis, E. M., McKay, K. E., Schultz, K. P., Newcorn, J. H., & Halperin, J. M. (2000). Parent-teacher concordance for DSM-IV attention-deficit/hyperactivity disorder in a clinic-referred sample. *Journal of the American Academy of Child and Adolescent Psychiatry, 39*(3), 308-313.

Murray, K. T., & Kochanska, G. (2002). Effortful control: Factor structure and relation to externalizing and internalizing behaviors. *Journal of Abnormal Child Psychology, 30*(5), 503-514.

Murray, D. W., Kollins, S. H., Hardy, K. K., Abikoff, H. B., Swanson, J. M., Cunningham, C., et al. (2007). Parent versus teacher ratings of attention-deficit/hyperactivity disorder symptoms in the preschoolers with attention-deficit/hyperactivity disorder treatment study (PATS). *Journal of Child and Adolescent Psychopharmacology, 17*(5), 605-620.

NICHD Early Child Care Research Network. (2003). Do children's attention processes mediate the link between family predictors and school readiness? *Developmental Psychology, 39*(3), 581-593.

Nigg, J. T., Goldsmith, H. H., & Sachek, J. (2004). Temperament and attention deficit hyperactivity disorder: The development of a multiple pathway model. *Journal of Clinical Child and Adolescent Psychology, 33*(1), 42-53.

Norman, G., & Breznitz, Z. (1992). Differences in ability to concentrate in first grade Israeli pupils of low and high socioeconomic status. *The Journal of Genetic Psychology, 153*(1), 5-17.

Olson, S. L., Sameroff, A. J., Kerr, D. C., Lopez, N. L., & Wellman, H. M. (2005). Developmental foundations of externalizing problems in young children: The role of effortful control. *Developmental and Psychopathology, 17*, 25-45.

Pelham, W. E., Fabiano, G. A., & Massetti, G. M. (2005). Evidence-based assessment of attention deficit hyperactivity disorder in children and adolescents. *Journal of Clinical Child and Adolescent Psychology, 34*(3), 449-476.

Posner, M. I., & Petersen, S. E. (1990). The attention system of the human brain. *Annual Review of Neuroscience, 13*, 25-42.

Power, T. J., Doherty, B. J., Panichelli-Mindel, S. M., Karustis, J. L., Eiraldi, R. B., Anastopoulos, A. D., et al. (1998). The predictive validity of parent and teacher reports of ADHD symptoms. *Journal of Psychopathology and Behavioral Assessment, 20*(1), 57-81.

Redick, T. S., & Engle, R. W. (2006). Working memory capacity and attention network test performance. *Applied Cognitive Psychology, 20*, 713-721.

Rothbart, M. K., Ahadi, S. A., Hershey, K. L., & Fisher, P. (2001). Investigations of temperament at three to seven years: The Children's Behavior Questionnaire. *Child Development, 72*(5), 1394-1408.

Rothbart, M. K., Ellis, L. K., Rueda, M. R., & Posner, M. I. (2003). Developing mechanisms of temperamental effortful control. *Journal of Personality, 71*(6), 1113-1143.

Rothbart, M. K., Sheese, B. E., & Posner, M. I. (2007). Executive attention and effortful control: Linking temperament, brain networks, and genes. *Child Development Perspectives, 1*(1), 2-7.

Sax, L., & Kautz, K. J. (2003). Who first suggests the diagnosis of attention-deficit/hyperactivity disorder? *Annals of Family Medicine, 1*(3), 171-174.

Sayal, K., & Taylor, E. (2005). Parent ratings of school behavior in children at risk of attention deficit/hyperactivity disorder. *Acta Psychiatrica Scandinavica, 111*(6), 460-465.

Schneider, H., & Eisenberg, D. (2006). Who receives diagnosis of attention-deficit/hyperactivity disorder in the United States elementary school population? *Pediatrics, 117*, 601-609.

Swanson, J. M., Casey, B. J., Nigg, J., Castellanos, F. X., Bolkow, N. D., & Taylor, E. (2004). Clinical and cognitive definitions of attention deficits in children with attention-deficit/hyperactivity disorder. In M. I. Posner (Ed.), *Cognitive neuroscience of attention* (pp. 430-445). New York: Guilford Press

Tripp, G., Schaughency, E. A., & Bronwyn, C. (2006). Parent and teacher rating scales in the evaluation of attention-deficit hyperactivity disorder: Contribution to diagnosis and differential diagnosis in clinically referred children. *Developmental and Behavioral Pediatrics, 27*(3), 209-218.

Wachs, T. D. (1979). Proximal experience and early cognitive intellectual development: The physical environment. *Merrill-Palmer Quarterly, 25*(1), 3-41.

Weatherholt, T. N., Harris, R. C., Burns, B. M., & Clement, C. (2006). Analysis of attention and analogical reasoning in children of poverty. *Journal of Applied Developmental Psychology, 27*(2), 125-135.

Weaver, B., Bédard, M., McAuliffe, J., & Parkari, M. (2009). Using the attention network test to predict driving test scores. *Accident Analysis and Prevention, 41*, 76-83.

Willcutt, E. G., Doyle, A. E., Nigg, J. T., Faraone, S. V., & Pennington, B. F. (2005). Validity of the executive function theory of attention-deficit/hyperactivity disorder: A meta-analytic review. *Biological Psychiatry, 57*, 1336-1346.

Associations Among Young Children's Temperament, Parents' Perceptions of Their Young Children, and Characteristics of the Parent-Young Child Relationship

Stephanie Aring & Kimberly Renk
University of Central Florida

Research has suggested that young children's temperament and parents' behaviors are related; however, few studies have examined variables that may help professionals who work with young children better understand this association. Therefore, this exploratory study examined parents' perceptions of their young children as a potential mediating variable in the association between characteristics of young children's temperament and the parent-young child relationship. Forty-nine parents of young children who ranged in age from 2- to 6-years and who were attending private preschool/daycare programs in a Southeastern state completed measures regarding the variables of interest. Correlational analyses indicated that these variables were related significantly. Further, regression analyses suggested that parents' positive perceptions predicted parents' involvement and communication. Regression analyses also suggested that parents' negative perceptions of their young children mediated the association between parent-young child relationship characteristics and young children's effortful control. These findings emphasized the importance of considering parents' perceptions of their young children in investigating the parent-young child relationship and young children's temperament.

Key Words: Parent, Young Child, Temperament, Perceptions, Relationship

Research has suggested that young children's temperament and parents' behaviors are interrelated (Calkins, Hungerford, & Dedmon, 2004; Rubin, Burgess, Dwyer, & Hastings, 2003). In many research studies, young children's temperament is thought to prompt parents to interact with their young children in certain ways (Collins, Maccoby, Steinberg, Hetherington, & Bornstein, 2000; O'Connor, 2002). For example, young children's difficult temperaments (e.g., they are fussy or hard to soothe) may be related to mothers' development of negative or unfavorable parenting behaviors (Bowlby, 1982).

All correspondence should be addressed to Kimberly Renk, Ph.D., University of Central Florida, Department of Psychology, P.O. Box 161390, Orlando, Florida 32816. Electronic mail may be sent to krenk@mail.ucf.edu.

It also is likely, however, that parents' behaviors in the context of their relationships with their young children are associated with changes in young children's temperament (Collins et al.; O'Connor). Thus, the association between young children's temperament and parents' behaviors is bidirectional in nature, as parents and young children often influence each other (Patterson, 1982). Although these associations are noted in the research literature, fewer studies examine variables that may help professionals who work with young children better understand this association.

In fact, parents' perceptions may be an important mediating variable in the association between these variables. Parents' perceptions may color their views of their young children as well as young children's views of themselves. Knowing that parents hold certain perceptions may prompt young children to exhibit emotions and behaviors that are consistent with these perceptions. For example, parents who are having to set more limits for their young children's behaviors may perceive their children more negatively. In turn, these negative perceptions may prompt parents to feel that their young children have less control over their own behaviors. Given that parents' perceptions may be useful in understanding the association between young children's temperament and characteristics of the parent-young child relationship, this study examines the associations among these variables.

Young Children's Temperament

When describing young children's functioning, their temperament (i.e., their individual predisposition toward emotional reactivity and self-regulation [Bates, Maslin, & Frankel, 1985] as well as their early-appearing behavioral approaches and emotional dispositions [Calkins et al., 2004]) often is considered. When describing young children's temperament, reactivity refers to children's ease of arousal when they are responding to their environments, whereas children's self-regulation refers to processes that modulate reactivity (Kagan, 2003). As temperament is conceptualized usually as being biologically based (Calkins et al.) and influenced by genes (Goldsmith et al., 1987), it often is considered to be innate and stable (Bates et al.). Nonetheless, young children also must develop the ability to process and regulate their reactions to sensory stimuli from their environments while maintaining their attention and remaining in a state of calm (DeGangi, 2000; Greenspan, 2007). This regulation allows young children to develop their ability to build relationships, exhibit appropriate behaviors, and acquire appropriate affect. Thus, temperament also may be influenced over time by young children's environmental experiences (Rothbart & Bates, 2006). Such findings would suggest that there is a bidirectional relationship between young children's temperament and their environments.

Further, young children's temperament is related to their interactions with other individuals. In particular, young children's temperament is related to how they react to others and how others react to them (Bates et al., 1985; Shaw et al., 1998). In fact, some researchers defined temperament in terms of different dimensions that represent young children's different response styles across contexts (e.g., Thomas, Chess, Birch, Hertzig, & Korn's [1963] nine dimensions). Further, Buss and Plomin (1975) considered temperament in terms of three dimensions (i.e., emotionality [distress], activity [behavioral arousal], and sociability [preference for being with others versus being alone]), all of which may be related to interactions that transpire with other individuals. Rothbart, Ahadi, Hershey, and Fisher (2001) also derived three broad dimensions of temperament that are applicable across cultures and that may be related to young children's interactions with others. These dimensions also appear to be related to different emotional and behavioral symptoms that young children may exhibit (e.g., Renk et al., in press). These dimensions include: Negative Affectivity (encompassing children's anger, discomfort, fear, sadness, and a negative loading for soothability), Surgency/Extraversion (encompassing children's activity level, high-intensity pleasure, impulsivity, and a negative loading for shyness), and Effortful Control (encompassing children's attentional focusing, inhibitory control, low-intensity pleasure, and perceptual sensitivity; Rothbart et al.).

Although children may be born with certain temperamental tendencies, research has further suggested that children's temperament is related to the parenting behaviors utilized by their mothers and fathers (Ge, Conger, & Elder, 1996; O'Connor, Deater-Deckard, Fulker, Rutter, & Plomin, 1998). For example, children who have difficult temperaments are more likely to have mothers who exhibit more negative affectivity and who have more nonaccepting attitudes toward their children (Webster-Stratton & Eyberg, 1982). Further, Webster-Stratton and Eyberg suggested that mothers' negative attitudes may result from the low levels of positive reinforcement that children who are temperamentally difficult provide to their mothers. Thus, the combination of young children's difficult temperament and negative parenting behaviors likely would promote problematic interactions between young children and their parents.

Although young children's temperament may prompt different behaviors from parents, parents' behaviors also may promote changes in young children's temperament (Collins et al., 2000; O'Connor, 2002). For example, certain parenting behaviors (e.g., power assertive behaviors) may contribute to young children's development of effortful control (Kochanska & Knaack, 2003; Spinrad et al., 2007) and other components of temperament. Parents, as well as other individuals, also may impose regulation on young children (Berger, 2005). For example, during the infant and toddler years, young children's emotions usually are regulated, at least somewhat, by their caregivers. As they move through development, young children move from using the regulation strategies of other individuals, such as their parents, to increasingly participating in the regulation and expression of their own emotions (Cole, Michel, & Teti, 1994). In fact, the match between young children's temperament and their parents' behaviors plays a significant role in the development of self-regulation (Thomas & Chess, 1977). Thus, it is likely that young children's temperament predicts parents' behavior and that parent-imposed regulation, in the context of the parent-young child relationship, predicts young children's temperament.

The Parent-Young Child Relationship

Given its association with young children's temperament, the importance of the parent-young child relationship cannot be understated. In fact, attachment theory (Ainsworth, Blehar, Waters, & Wall, 1978; Bowlby, 1969; Carlson & Sroufe, 1995), social learning theory (Bandura, 1986, 1997; Patterson, DeBaryshe, & Ramsey, 1989), and the goodness of fit model (Thomas, Chess, & Birch, 1968), among other theories, all stress the importance of young children's relationships with their parents (or other primary caregivers) for young children's development. As there are so many developmental milestones that young children must master (e.g., goal-directed behavior, cognitive representational abilities, regulation of emotions and behaviors; Jennings, 2004), parents and young children may find it challenging to build a positive relationship with one another (e.g., Renk, Klein, Oliveros, & McKinney, 2006). Nonetheless, continuous interactions between parents and their young children allow their relationship to develop, as both parents and their young children have an effect on and change "the other's behaviors and expectations in an ongoing feedback loop" (NICHD Early Child Care Research Network, 2004, p. 44). Thus, the parent-young child relationship depends on the characteristics of both parents and their young children.

Consistently, research has demonstrated that characteristics of the parent-young child relationship are important to young children's functioning (e.g., Ainsworth et al., 1978; Baumrind, 1968; Bowlby, 1969; Bradley & Corwyn, 2005). Certain parenting behaviors are known to promote positive outcomes for children. In particular, parents who build a warm relationship that incorporates appropriate communication, limit setting, and autonomy granting are most likely to promote such positive outcomes (Baumrind, 1968). Such parents sometimes are labeled with the term 'authoritative' (Baumrind, 1991). In other cases, however, harsh parenting behaviors are used, with children who exhibit difficult behaviors being at risk for such parenting behaviors (Eisenberg et al., 1999; Patterson, 1982). Harsh parenting includes generally behaviors that are emotionally inconsistent, emotionally negative, coercive, overreactive, angry, hostile, controlling, and authoritarian (Arnold, O'Leary, Wolff, & Acker, 1993; Deater-Deckard & Dodge, 1997; Scaramella & Leve, 2004). Unfortunately, harsh parenting behavior can lead to future emotional and behavioral problems for children. These problems may include externalizing disorders (Shaw, Owens, Giovanelli, & Winslow, 2001), conduct problems at school (Eisenberg et al., 1999), and aggression and antisocial behavior (Patterson, 1982).

When parents' harsh behaviors and communication are coupled with their children's negative emotional reactivity, a reciprocally reinforcing coercive relationship can develop over time (Keenan & Shaw, 1995; Patterson, 1982). For example, the Early Childhood Coercion Model (Scaramella & Leve, 2004) suggested that coercive cycles of interactions in the parent-child relationship can develop during the preschool years from negative interactions that began during the infancy and toddler years. These types of relationship characteristics can inhibit young children's development for a variety of reasons. For example, parents' efforts to socialize their young children may be impeded because they are too aroused emotionally, young children may be provided with a poor model for appropriate regulation behaviors, and young children (especially those who are highly reactive) may be provided with an environment that is too arousing for them to be able to call on appropriate strategies (Chang, Schwartz, Dodge, & McBride-Change, 2003; Eisenberg et al., 1999; NICHD Early Child Care Research Network, 2004; Scaramella & Leve). Thus, it is likely that characteristics of the relationship that develops between parents and their young children are linked closely to the level of functioning that is achieved by young children. As a result, gaining further understanding of the association between young children's temperament and characteristics of the parent-young child relationship is warranted.

Parents' Perceptions

Although the association between young children's temperament and characteristics of the parent-young child relationship has been documented, identification of potential mediators in this relationship may be needed to fully understand this association. For example, professionals who work with young children may wonder how or why young children's temperament and parent-young child relationship characteristics are related. In fact, parents' perceptions of their children may play an important role in how parents interact with their young children and in young children's temperament. In particular, such perceptions may serve as an important mediator in the association between these variables. As noted in Phares and Renk (1998), perceptions are cognitive and emotional representations of the external world. In other words, parents' perceptions can be conceptualized as their overall opinion, feelings, or interpretations regarding their children. Further, consistent with schema theory (e.g., Fiske & Taylor, 1984), parents also may use relational schemas based on their consistent relationship patterns with their children to interpret their children's behavior (Baldwin, 1992). Thus, if parents' perceived their young children positively, they may interact more positively with them and rate their emotional and behavioral tendencies more positively. In contrast, if parents' perceived their young children negatively, they may interact more negatively with them and rate their emotional and behavioral tendencies more negatively.

Attribution theory may provide other useful clues to the importance of parents' perceptions of their children. According to attribution theory, attributions are what individuals use to explain events in their lives. Individuals can make internal attributions, assigning causality to factors within themselves, or external attributions, assigning causality to factors outside themselves or out of their control (Heider, 1958). In the context of the parent-young child relationship, parents make inferences about the cause of their young children's behavior, attributing the behavior to internal factors (e.g., disposition and intention) or external factors (e.g., situational stressors or developmental limits in knowledge and ability; Dix, Ruble, Grusec, & Nixon, 1986). More specifically, Hayes and Ju (1995) defined parental attributions as "verbal-cognitive rules about sources of child misbehavior that are used to guide discipline efforts" (p. 31). In fact, many studies noted a relationship between parental attributions and parents' behavior (e.g., Baden & Howe, 1992; Bugental, Blue, & Cruzcosa, 1989; Dix & Lochman, 1990; Snyder, Cramer, Afrank, & Patterson, 2005). Parents' perceptions of their children may operate in a similar fashion.

Consistently, research has shown a strong relationship between parents' behaviors toward their children and parents' perceptions. For example, Strassberg (1995) indicated that parents of children with behavior problems respond to and interpret their children's behavior more negatively, regardless of these children's cooperative, ambiguous, or resistant behavior responses. In addition, other research suggested that parents' behavior is related to their perceptions of their children's behavior. In particular, parents' perceptions and attributions are linked to child abuse (Bugental et al., 1989), child discipline (Dix & Lochman, 1990), and socialization of children (Dix & Grusec, 1985) as well as to parents' ratings of children's behavior problems (Renk, in press). Further, Bugental and Shennum (1984) indicated that parents who expect negative behavior from their children tend to react negatively to their children. These reactions from parents subsequently elicit negative reactions from their children and result in the reinforcement of the parents' prior attributions. Given these findings, it is likely that parents' perceptions of their young children may be used to explain the association between young children's temperament and characteristics of the parent-young child relationship.

The Current Study

Although the association between young children's temperament and the characteristics of the parent-young child relationship has been documented (Collins et al., 2000; O'Connor, 2002), parents' perceptions of their young children have not been examined as a potential mediating variable that could further explain this association. As a result, this study examined the associations among young children's temperament, parents' perceptions of their young children, and characteristics of the parent-young child relationship. It was anticipated that these variables would be related significantly. Further, it was hypothesized that young children's temperament and parents' perceptions would predict characteristics of the parent-young child relationship and that parents' perceptions would mediate the relationship between young children's temperament and these relationship characteristics. Finally, given the potential bidirectional relationship between young children's temperament and parent-young child relationship characteristics, it was hypothesized that characteristics of the parent-young child relationship and parents' perceptions of their young children would predict young children's temperament. In turn, it was anticipated that parents' perceptions would mediate the association between characteristics of the parent-young child relationship and young children's temperament.

Method

Participants. The parents of 49 young children who ranged in age from 2 to 6 years provided ratings of their young children's temperaments, their perceptions of their young children, and characteristics of their relationships with their young children. Of these parents, 39 (79.6%) were mothers, 9 (18.4%) were fathers, and one parent (2.0%) did not indicate their sex. The mean age of these parents was 35.83 years ($SD = 6.82$ years). The majority of these parents indicated that they were married (81.6%), with the remainder endorsing a different relationship status (i.e., 10.2% were never married, 4.2% were divorced or separated, 2.0% had some other relationship status, and 2.0% did not report information about their relationship status). With regard to education, the majority of parents had attained a college degree (65.3%). An additional 16.3% of parents had completed some college, 16.3% had completed graduate school, and 2% failed to provide their level of education. On average, parents indicated that they fell within the 'Technician, Semiprofessional, and Small Business Owner' category of Hollingshead's (1975) Four Factor Index of Social Status. Over half of the sample (57.1%) made $65,000 or more per year, with 28.6% making below $65,000 per year and 14.3% not providing their income.

The young children of these parents were enrolled in two private preschool/daycare programs in the central region of a Southeastern state. With regard to the young children that were rated, 18 (36.7%) were males, 30 (61.2%) were females, and one (2.0%) young child did not have their sex indicated. The majority of these young children were Caucasian (69.4%). The remainder of the young children varied in their ethnic backgrounds (i.e., 12.2% Hispanic, 10.2% Asian/Pacific Islander, 4.1% African American, 2.0% other, and 2.0% not provided). The mean age of these young children was 3.63 years ($SD = 0.94$ years).

Measures. *Young Children's Temperament.* Young children's temperament was measured using the Very Short Form of the *Children's Behavior Questionnaire* (CBQ; Putnam & Rothbart, 2006; Rothbart et al., 2001). This instrument has three factors that assess broad dimensions of temperament (as discussed previously). These dimensions are Surgency/Extraversion, Negative Affectivity, and Effortful Control. This measure consists of 36 items, each rated from *extremely untrue of your child* (1) to *extremely true of your child* (7). Parents also are given a *not applicable* (0) response option. The CBQ had an overall internal consistency reliability coefficient of .77 in a previous study. It also had good convergent validity in this previous study (Rothbart et al.). Putnam and Rothbart also noted that the Very Short Form of the CBQ demonstrates satisfactory internal consistency (with *alpha* coefficients ranging from .62 to .78) and criterion validity as well as satisfactory longitudinal stability and cross-informant agreement.

   The Parent-Young Child Relationship. Characteristics of parents' relationship with their young children were measured using specific subscales of the *Parent-Child Relationship Inventory* (PCRI; Gerard, 1994). The PCRI contains 78 items that parents rate using a scale ranging from *strongly agree* (1) to *strongly disagree* (4). The measure has seven subscales that examine specific aspects of the parent-child relationship. For the current study, the Involvement, Communication, Limit Setting, and Autonomy Granting subscales were utilized, as these subscales measure more interactive aspects of the parent-young child relationship. The Involvement subscale measures the amount of interaction and knowledge that parents have with regard to their children. The Communication subscale measures parents' awareness of their ability to communicate with their children. The Limit Setting subscale measures the discipline practices utilized by parents and the effectiveness of these practices, and the Autonomy Granting subscale measures parents' ability to promote their children's independence. The PCRI demonstrated good internal consistency (with Cronbach *alpha*s ranging from .76 to .88 for the subscales used in this study) and test-retest reliability (with reliability coefficients ranging from .68 to .93 over one week for the subscales used in this study). It also had adequate content, construct, and predictive validity in previous studies (Gerard, 1994).

   Parents' Perceptions. The *Perceptions of Parents Scale-Parent Version* (POP; Phares & Renk, 1998) was completed by parents as a measure of their own positive and negative perceptions of their young children. The POP has two scales, Positive Affect and Negative Affect, with higher scores reflecting higher levels of each type of perception. There are a total of 15 items, each rated from *not at all or never* (1) to *extremely or always* (6). Each item requires parents to rate how they feel about their children. This measure was designed originally to measure adolescents' perceptions of their mothers and fathers and showed strong psychometric properties in this format. For example, the internal consistency for the Positive Affect scale (.96-.97 for mothers and .97-.98 for fathers) and the Negative Affective scale (.81 for mothers and .83-.84 for fathers) were both high. For this study, a reworded version of this measure was used to allow parents to rate their perceptions of their children. The POP was used in this manner in other studies and demonstrated strong psychometric properties in this format. For example, the internal consistency for the Positive Affect scale (.86) and the Negative Affect scale (.77) were both high (Renk, Roddenberry, Oliveros, & Sieger, 2007).

Demographics. Parents also completed a brief questionnaire regarding demographics information. The demographics questionnaire asked parents to provide information about themselves and their child's other parent regarding their age, occupation, ethnicity, and other related characteristics.

Procedure. Following the receipt of IRB approval, parents were recruited from two private preschool/daycare centers in the central region of a Southeastern state. Data collection involved distributing questionnaire packets that included the measures described above, as well as other measures not examined here, to parents who expressed interest in participating in the study at their respective preschool/daycare center. Parents were permitted to complete the surveys at home and return them upon completion to their child's center in a sealed envelope for the investigators to collect. A detailed sheet containing instructions for completing the questionnaires was included with the packet. This sheet also provided contact information for the investigators in the event that parents had questions about any of the questionnaires. A consent form was included with the packet to ensure that parents understood that their participation was completely voluntary and that their answers would remain confidential. In addition, parents were given a debriefing form upon completion of the questionnaire packet to explain the purpose of this study and provide relevant research references.

Results

Descriptive statistics. To put the results of the sample examined in this study into context, descriptive statistics (i.e., means and standard deviations) were calculated and examined in terms of the relative range available for each measure. Refer to Table 1 for the descriptive statistics. In terms of characteristics of the parent-young child relationship, parents reported relatively high levels of involvement, communication, limit setting, and autonomy granting with their young children. With regard to parents' perceptions of their young children, parents endorsed relatively high levels of positive perceptions and low levels of negative perceptions. Finally, with regard to children's temperament, parents endorsed moderate levels of surgency, lower levels of negative affectivity, and relatively high levels of effortful control in their young children.

Correlational analyses. To examine the associations among characteristics of the parent-young child relationship, parents' perceptions of their young children, and young children's temperament in the sample examined for this study, correlational analyses were examined. Refer to Table 2 for these correlations. Correlational analyses in this study suggested that parents' ratings of their

Table 1
Descriptive Statistics for Study Variables

Variable	Range	M	SD
Relationship Characteristics			
1. Involvement	14-56	28.27	3.06
2. Communication	9-36	26.38	2.33
3. Limit Setting	12-48	31.13	2.65
4. Autonomy Granting	10-40	24.85	3.36
Parents' Perceptions			
5. Positive Perceptions	1-6	5.63	.42
6. Negative Perceptions	1-6	2.14	.46
Young Children's Temperament			
7. Negative Affectivity	0-84	44.79	9.39
8. Surgency	0-84	52.79	9.67
9. Effortful Control	0-84	64.52	8.01

involvement with their young children were negatively correlated with parents' positive perceptions of their young children, $r = -.49, p < .001$. In contrast, parents' communication with their young children was related significantly and positively to parents' positive perceptions of their young children, $r = .50, p < .001$. Further, parents' limit setting was related significantly and negatively to parents' negative perceptions of their young children, $r = -.42, p < .01$, but significantly and positively to young children's effortful control, $r = .34, p < .05$. Parents' involvement with their young children also was related significantly and positively to young children's negative affectivity, $r = .30 \, p < .05$. Further, parents' positive perceptions of their young children were related significantly and negatively to their young children's negative affectivity, $r = -.35, p < .05$, and parents' negative perceptions of their young children were related significantly and negatively to young children's effortful control, $r = -.56, p < .001$. Thus, these variables demonstrated significant correlations.

   Regression analyses.   To examine the predictive relationships among characteristics of the parent-young child relationship, parents' perceptions of their young children, and young children's temperament, a bidirectional approach was used. First, because the research literature suggested that young children's temperament may predict certain characteristics of the parent-young child relationship (e.g., Ge et al., 1996; O'Connor et al., 1998), young children's temperament was used as the predictor variables in one set of regression equations, and relationship characteristics were used as criterion variables. Second, because the research literature suggested that characteristics of the parent-young child relationship may shape young children's temperament (Collins et al., 2000; O'Connor, 2002), relationship characteristics were used as predictor variables in a second set of regression equations, and young children's temperaments were used as criterion variables. In both cases, parents' perceptions were included for examination as potential mediators.

Young children's temperament and parents' perceptions as predictors of parent-young child relationship characteristics. To examine the predictive value of young children's temperament and parents' perceptions in predicting characteristics of the parent-young child relationship, a series of hierarchical regression equations were conducted (i.e., one for each parent-young child relationship characteristic examined with the sample in this study). In each equation, young children's temperament was entered in Block 1 and parents' perceptions were entered in Block 2 (so that the amount of incremental variance could be examined). See Table 3 for these analyses.

For parents' involvement with their young children, the regression equation was not significant in Block 1, $F (3, 44) = 2.00$, $p > .05$. With the addition of parents' perceptions in Block 2, the regression equation became significant, $F (5, 42) = 3.85$, $p < .01$, however. In this block, parents' positive perceptions ($p < .001$) served as a significant predictor. Thus, parents' positive perceptions

Table 2

Correlations Among Study Variables

Variables	1	2	3	4	5	6	7	8	9
Relationship Characteristics									
1. Involvement	-								
2. Communication	-.24	-							
3. Limit Setting	-.05	.47***	-						
4. Autonomy Granting	-.08	.00	.07	-					
Parents' Perceptions									
5. Positive Perceptions	-.49***	.50***	.28	-.22	-				
6. Negative Perceptions	.09	-.21	-.42**	.28	-.53***	-			
Young Children's Temperament									
7. Negative Affectivity	.30*	-.02	-.09	.14	-.35*	.24	-		
8. Surgency	-.20	.25	.00	-.18	.28	-.18	-.13	-	
9. Effortful Control	-.04	.17	.34*	-.26	.22	-.56***	-.05	.01	-

Note. *$p < .05$ **$p < .01$ ***$p < .001$

Table 3

Young Children's Temperament and Parents' Perceptions as Predictors of Parent-Young Child Characteristics

Variable	SEB	β	t
Involvement			
Block 1. F (3, 44) = 2.00, p > .05, r2 = .12			
Negative Affectivity	.05	.28	1.97
Surgency	.05	-.17	-1.16
Effortful Control	.05	-.03	-.19
Block 2. F (5, 42) = 3.85, p < .01, r2 = .31			
Negative Affectivity	.05	.17	1.26
Surgency	.04	-.08	-.60
Effortful Control	.06	-.08	-.52
Positive Perceptions	1.16	-.55	-3.44***
Negative Perceptions	1.22	-.31	-1.69
Communication			
Block 1. F (3, 44) = 1.51, p > .05, r2 = .09			
Negative Affectivity	.04	.02	.12
Surgency	.04	.25	1.75
Effortful Control	.04	.17	1.19
Block 2. F (5, 42) = 3.75, p < .01, r2 = .31			
Negative Affectivity	.03	.16	1.16
Surgency	.03	.14	1.06
Effortful Control	.05	.14	.91
Positive Perceptions	.89	.57	3.55***
Negative Perceptions	.93	.16	.90
Limit Setting			
Block 1. F (3, 44) = 1.97, p > .05, r2 = .12			
Negative Affectivity	.04	-.08	-.53
Surgency	.04	-.01	-.07
Effortful Control	.05	.33	2.34*
Block 2. F (5, 42) = 2.10, p > .05, r2 = .20			
Negative Affectivity	.04	.02	.11
Surgency	.04	-.08	-.55
Effortful Control	.06	.15	.89
Positive Perceptions	1.08	.12	.69
Negative Perceptions	1.14	-.28	-1.45
Autonomy Granting			
Block 1. F (3, 44) = 1.80, p < .05, r2 = .11			
Negative Affectivity	.05	.11	.77
Surgency	.05	-.16	-1.12
Effortful Control	.06	-.25	-1.77
Block 2. F (5, 42) = 1.80, p < .05, r2 = .12			
Negative Affectivity	.06	.07	.46
Surgency	.05	-.13	-.87
Effortful Control	.07	-.18	-1.02
Positive Perceptions	1.44	-.06	-.31
Negative Perceptions	1.51	.11	.52

Note.   *p < .05   **p < .01   ***p < .001

appeared to be important for parents' involvement with their young children, with parents who held less positive perceptions becoming more involved with their young children.

For parents' communication with their young children, the regression equation was not significant in Block 1, $F\ (3, 44) = 1.51$, $p > .05$. With the addition of parents' perceptions in Block 2, the regression equation became significant, $F\ (5, 42) = 3.75$, $p < .01$, however. In this block, only parents' positive perceptions ($p < .001$) served as a significant predictor. Thus, again, parents' positive perceptions appeared to be important for parents' communication with their young children. In particular, parents who held more positive perceptions endorsed higher levels of communication with their young children.

For parents' limit setting behaviors, the regression equation was not significant in Block 1, $F\ (3, 44) = 1.97$, $p > .05$. With the addition of parents' perceptions in Block 2, the regression equation also was not significant, $F\ (5, 42) = 2.10$, $p > .05$. Thus, neither young children's temperament nor parents' perceptions appeared to be particularly important for parents' limit setting behaviors in the parent-young child relationship.

For parents' autonomy granting, the regression equation was not significant in Block 1, $F\ (3, 44) = 1.80$, $p > .05$. With the addition of parents' perceptions in Block 2, the regression equation also was not significant, $F\ (5, 42) = 1.17$, $p > .05$. Thus, neither young children's temperament nor parents' perceptions appeared to be particularly important for parents' autonomy granting behaviors in the parent-young child relationship.

If parents' perceptions were serving as a mediator in the relationship between young children's temperament and characteristics of the parent-young child relationship, a characteristic pattern of results would have been noted (Baron & Kenny, 1986). First, young children's temperament would have served as a significant predictor in Block 1. Then, with the addition of parents' perceptions into the regression equations, young children's temperament would have exhibited an attenuated association with the parent-young child relationship characteristics, and parents' perceptions would have been a significant predictor. Given that none of the regression equations showed this pattern typical of mediation, parents' perceptions were not examined further as mediators in the association between young children's temperament and parent-young child relationship characteristics.

Parent-young child relationship characteristics and parents' perceptions as predictors of children's temperament. To examine the predictive value of characteristics of the parent-young child relationship and parents' perceptions in predicting young children's temperament, a second series of hierarchical regression equations were conducted (i.e., one for each temperament dimension examined). In each equation, characteristics of the parent-young child relationship were entered in Block 1 and parents' perceptions were entered in Block 2 (so that the amount of incremental variance could be examined). See Table 4 for these results.

For young children's negative affectivity, the regression equation was not significant in Block 1, F (4, 43) = 1.74, $p > .05$. With the addition of parents' perceptions in Block 2, the regression equation also was not significant, F (6, 41) = 1.61, $p > .05$. Thus, neither characteristics of the parent-young child relationship nor parents' perceptions appeared to be important predictors of young children's negative affectivity (e.g., their experience of different emotions, such as anger, discomfort, fear, and sadness).

For young children's surgency, the regression equation was not significant in Block 1, F (4, 43) = 1.63, $p > .05$. With the addition of parents' perceptions in Block 2, the regression equation also was not significant, F (6, 41) = 1.18, $p > .05$. Thus, neither characteristics of the parent-young child relationship nor parents' perceptions appeared to be important predictors of young children's surgency (e.g., their activity level and level of engagement with activities).

For young children's effortful control, the regression equation was significant in Block 1, F (4, 43) = 2.61, $p < .05$. In this Block, parents' limit setting and autonomy granting served as significant ($p < .05$) predictors. With the addition of parents' perceptions in Block 2, the regression equation remained significant, F (6, 41) = 4.04, $p < .01$. In this block, parents' limit setting and autonomy granting were no longer significant; however, parents' negative perceptions ($p < .01$) served as a significant predictor of young children's effortful control (e.g., their attentional focusing, inhibitory control, low-intensity pleasure, and perceptual sensitivity).

Given the pattern of relationships in these regression equations, parents' perceptions may serve as a mediator in the relationship between characteristics of the parent-young child relationship and young children's effortful control. To confirm that parents' perceptions do mediate this relationship, additional regression analyses were conducted. Based on Baron and Kenny (1986), evidence of a mediational model would require several findings. First, the predictor variable (i.e., characteristics of the parent-young child relationship) would have to predict the mediator (i.e., parents' perceptions) and the criterion variable (i.e., young children's effortful control). The mediator also would have to predict the criterion variable in an equation in the context of the predictor variable. Once the mediator is included in a prediction equation examining the main predictor and criterion, the relationship between the predictor and the criterion would no longer be significant (as already noted above). See Table 5 for a presentation of the regression analyses.

For the first set of regression equations necessary to examine Baron and Kenny's (1986) prescription for mediation, characteristics of the parent-young child relationship were used as predictors in regression equations predicting parents' positive and negative perceptions of their young children. With regard to positive perceptions, parent-young child relationship characteristics predicted

Table 4

Parent-Young Child Relationship Characteristics and Parents' Perceptions as Predictors of Young Children's Temperament

Variable	SEB	β	t
Negative Affectivity			
Block 1. F (4, 43) = 1.74, p > .05, r2 = .14			
Involvement	.45	.34	2.32*
Communication	.67	.12	.75
Limit Setting	.57	-.15	-.91
Autonomy Granting	.40	.18	1.26
Block 2. F (6, 41) = 1.61, p > .05, r2 = .19			
Involvement	.52	.22	1.30
Communication	.73	.22	1.20
Limit Setting	.63	-.09	-.50
Autonomy Granting	.43	.09	.59
Positive Perceptions	4.89	-.27	-1.23
Negative Perceptions	3.91	.06	.32
Surgency			
Block 1. F (4, 43) = 1.63, p > .05, r2 = .13			
Involvement	.47	-.26	-1.07
Communication	.69	.27	1.63
Limit Setting	.59	-.12	-.73
Autonomy Granting	.41	-.18	-1.27
Block 2. F (6, 41) = 1.18, p > .05, r2 = .15			
Involvement	.55	-.13	-.75
Communication	.78	.26	1.40
Limit Setting	.66	-.18	-.98
Autonomy Granting	.45	-.13	-.84
Positive Perceptions	5.17	.04	.16
Negative Perceptions	4.14	-.13	-.66
Effortful Control			
Block 1. F (4, 43) = 2.61, p < .05, r2 = .20			
Involvement	.37	-.05	-.35
Communication	.55	-.01	-.03
Limit Setting	.47	.36	2.29*
Autonomy Granting	.33	-.29	-2.09*
Block 2. F (6, 41) = 4.04, p < .01, r2 = .37			
Involvement	.39	-.10	-.64
Communication	.55	.09	.57
Limit Setting	.47	.14	.87
Autonomy Granting	.32	-.17	-1.27
Positive Perceptions	3.68	-.24	-1.24
Negative Perceptions	2.94	-.56	-3.36**

Note. *p < .05   **p < .01   ***p < .001

Table 5

Summary of Mediation Regressions

Variable	SEB	β	t
Predictor and Criterion			
Parent-Young Child Interaction and Effortful Control. F (4, 43) = 2.61, p < .05, r2 = .20			
Involvement	.37	-.05	-.35
Communication	.55	-.01	-.03
Limit Setting	.47	.36	2.29*
Autonomy Granting	.33	-.29	-2.09*
Predictor and Mediator			
Parent-Young Child Interaction and Positive Perception. F (4, 43) = 9.43, p < .001, r2 = .47			
Involvement	.02	-.42	-3.66***
Communication	.02	.35	2.68**
Limit Setting	.02	.11	.89
Autonomy Granting	.01	-.26	-2.28*
Parent-Young Child Interaction and Negative Perception. F (4, 43) = 4.12, p < .01, r2 = .28			
Involvement	.02	.10	.75
Communication	.03	.02	.14
Limit Setting	.03	-.44	-3.00**
Autonomy Granting	.02	.32	2.44*
Predictor, Mediator, and Criterion (Effortful Control)			
Block 1. F (4, 43) = 2.61, p < .05, r2 = .20			
Involvement	.37	-.05	-.35
Communication	.55	-.01	-.03
Limit Setting	.47	.36	2.29*
Autonomy Granting	.33	-.29	-2.09*
Block 2. F (6, 41) = 4.04, p < .01, r2 = .37			
Involvement	.39	-.10	-.64
Communication	.55	.09	.57
Limit Setting	.47	.14	.87
Autonomy Granting	.32	-.17	-1.27
Positive Perceptions	3.68	-.24	-1.24
Negative Perceptions	2.94	-.56	-3.36**

Note.   *p < .05   **p < .01   ***p < .001

significantly positive perceptions, F (4, 43) = 9.43, $p < .001$. In this equation, parents' involvement with their young children ($p < .001$), parents' communication with their young children ($p < .01$), and parents' autonomy granting ($p < .05$) served as significant individual predictors. With regard to negative perceptions, parent-young child relationship characteristics significantly predicted negative perceptions, F (4, 43) = 4.12, $p < .01$. In this equation, parents' limit setting ($p < .01$) and autonomy granting ($p < .05$) served as significant predictors. Thus, characteristics of parent-young child relationships predicted significantly parents' perceptions of their young children.

For the second set of regression equations needed to confirm mediation, characteristics of the parent-young child relationship were used as predictors in a regression equation predicting young children's effortful control. Parent-young child relationship characteristics predicted significantly parents' ratings of their young children's effortful control, F (4, 43) = 2.61, $p < .05$, with parents' limit setting and autonomy granting serving as significant ($p < .05$) individual predictors. In conjunction with the initial hierarchical regression analysis reported, this pattern of findings suggested that parents' negative perceptions served as a mediator in the relationship between characteristics of the parent-young child relationship and parents' ratings of their young children's effort control.

Discussion

This study examined the associations among young children's temperament, parents' perceptions of their young children, and characteristics of the parent-young child relationship. Previous research suggested that young children's temperament and parents' behavior are interrelated (Calkins et al., 2004; Rubin et al., 2003). Previous research also suggested that interactions in the context of the parent-child relationship and parents' attributions are interrelated and may shape children's behavior (e.g., Baden & Howe, 1992; Bugental et al., 1989; Dix & Lochman, 1990; Snyder et al., 2005). Consistent with this previous research, the findings of this study suggested that there is indeed a bidirectional association between young children's temperament and characteristics of the parent-young child relationship. Thus, both young children's temperament and characteristics of the parent-young child relationship may be important in influencing each other and in shaping the outcomes experienced by young children. Further, parents' perceptions may help to explain this association between characteristics of the parent-young child relationship and young children's temperament. These perceptions may color parents' views of their young children and young children's views of themselves, perhaps prompting young children to exhibit emotions and behaviors that are consistent with these views.

Generally, the findings of this study confirmed results described in previous research examining the associations between characteristics of the parent-young child relationship and young children's temperament. In particular, parents' involvement was related significantly and positively to young children's negative affectivity (e.g., children's anger, discomfort, fear, and sadness), whereas parents' limit setting was related significantly and positively to young children's effortful control (e.g., encompassing children's attentional focusing, inhibitory control, low-intensity pleasure, and perceptual sensitivity; Rothbart et al., 2001). Regression analyses also suggested that specific characteristics of young children's temperament would predict individually different characteristics of the parent-young child relationship. These findings suggested that parents' use of limit setting may facilitate young children's acquisition of their own regulation skills (Cole et al., 1994), whereas parents' communication with their young children may decrease young children's overactivity and promote more positive outcomes (Baumrind, 1968).

One of the new contributions of this study is the inclusion of parents' perceptions as a mediating variable in the context of the association between young children's temperament and characteristics of the parent-young child relationship. In particular, parents' involvement was related significantly and negatively to parents' positive perceptions of their young children, whereas parents' communication was related significantly and positively to parents' positive perceptions of their young children. Given these relationships, it may be the case that parents who felt the need to be more involved with their young children ultimately developed less positive perceptions of their children, whereas those parents who felt that they communicated well with their young children ultimately had more positive perceptions. Further, parents' limit setting was related significantly and negatively to parents' negative perception of their young children. This relationship may suggest that parents who were using limit setting more effectively ultimately developed less negative perceptions of their young children. Given these findings, it may be the case that parents' communication and limit setting in the context of their relationship with their young children serve as protective factors for parents' perceptions of their young children (e.g., Baumrind, 1968). Thus, by promoting effective communication and limit setting skills for parents, professionals who work with young children and their families may facilitate more positive and less negative perceptions for parents of young children. Such changes in perceptions may promote subsequently positive outcomes for families in general and for young children in particular. Such potential treatment outcomes should be examined in future research.

Parents' perceptions also were related to parents' ratings of young children's temperament. With regard to parents' perceptions of their young children, parents' positive perceptions were related significantly and negatively to young children's negative affectivity, and parents' negative perceptions of their young children were related significantly and negatively to young children's effortful control. Thus, specific characteristics of the parent-young child relationship have important associations with parents' perceptions of their young children. Such findings may suggest that parents may hold more positive perceptions of their young children when they exhibit lower degrees of negative emotionality. Further, parents may hold less negative perceptions of their young children when they perceive their young children to be maintaining control over their own behaviors. Thus, consistent with schema theory (e.g., Fiske & Taylor, 1984) and other research (e.g., Baldwin, 1992), those parents who hold more positive and less negative perceptions of their young children may form a mental representation of their young children that fosters a recognition of their young children's beneficial behaviors over time.

Generally, the regression analyses in this study suggesteed that parents' perceptions of their young children mediate the relationship between characteristics of the parent-young child relationship and young children's temperament. In particular, parents' communication, involvement, and autonomy granting predicted their positive perceptions of their young children. Further, parents' limit setting and autonomy granting predicted their negative perceptions of their young children as well as young children's effortful control. Finally, when examining characteristics of the parent-young child relationship and parents' perceptions collectively, parents' limit setting and autonomy granting were no longer significant predictors of young children's effortful control, whereas parents' negative perceptions were a significant predictor of young children's effortful control. Thus, similar to the pattern of behavior described by Patterson's (1982) coercion cycle and the model proposed by Scaramella and Leve (2004), parents' inability to set limits and grant autonomy predicted young children's difficulties with controlling their actions and focusing their attention. In addition, however, such behaviors predicted parents' negative perceptions of their young children. These negative perceptions may have colored parents' views of their young children, in that these parents rated their young children's behaviors as being more problematic.

The findings of this study should be interpreted in the context of its limitations. First, the main limitation is a potential lack of generalizability of these findings to parents who have characteristics different from those of the relatively homogeneous sample examined in this study. In particular, the sample for this study consisted primarily of Caucasian parents who were relatively well educated, had a sufficient income, and were able to have their young children attend private preschool/daycare centers. These characteristics of this sample may have decreased external validity in relation to parents who have other characteristics not represented here. Second, a sample size of 49 parents may have prevented there from being a sufficient degree of power to detect true relationships that may exist among the variables of interest in this study. Further, more mothers than fathers participated in this study, preventing an examination of sex differences for the associations of interest. Finally, this study relied on parents' self-report ratings, which cannot be assumed to be completely accurate.   In particular, parents' self-reports may have been subject to memory or other biases or to parents' tendency to respond in a socially desirable manner. Further, the variables examined here may have demonstrated a relationship simply because one parent completed measures assessing each of the variables. As a result, future research would benefit from the use of direct observation of relationships between parents and their young children in addition to the rating scales used in this study so that a more thorough and objective view of these variables could be obtained. Further, a longitudinal design that examines the variables of interest in this study may help to describe the potential for causal relationships among these variables (e.g., do characteristics of the parent-young child relationship shape young children's temperament over time?).

Despite these limitations, the results of this study have added to the literature concerning characteristics of the parent-young child relationship, parents' perceptions of their young children, and young children's temperament. The associations among the variables examined in this study may give insight to professionals working with troubled young children and their families on possible points of intervention. First, interventions that focus on parents' relationships with their young children as well as their perceptions of their young children may be particularly helpful in changing the trajectory of young children's emotions and behaviors. By helping improve parents' relationships with their children and their perceptions, many other aspects of parenting may be affected positively. Such improvements may promote positive changes in young children's emotions and behaviors and ultimately break the coercive cycle that may occur between parents and their young children (Patterson, 1982). These improvements will likely lead to parents feeling more satisfied with their role as a parent, using more positive parenting behaviors, having more positive and less negative perceptions of their young children, and promoting positive outcomes for their young children.

References

Ainsworth, M. D. S., Blehar, M. C., Waters, E., & Wall, S. (1978). *Patterns of attachment: A psychological study of the strange situation.* Hillsdale, NJ: Erlbaum.

Arnold, D., O'Leary, S., Wolff, L., & Acker, M. (1993). The parenting scale: A measure of dysfunctional parenting in discipline situations. *Psychological Assessment, 5,* 137-144.

Baden, A. D., & Howe, G. W. (1992). Mothers' attributions and expectancies regarding their conduct-disordered children. *Journal of Abnormal Child Psychology, 20,* 467-485.

Baldwin, M. W. (1992). Relational schemas and the processing of social information. *Psychological Bulletin, 112,* 461-484.

Bandura, A. (1986). *Social foundations of thought and action: A social cognitive theory.* Upper Saddle River, NJ: Prentice-Hall, Inc.

Bandura, A. (1997). *Self-efficacy: The exercise of control.* New York: Freeman.

Baron, R. M., & Kenny, D. A. (1986). The moderator-mediator variable distinction in social psychological research: Conceptual, strategic, and statistical considerations. *Journal of Personality and Social Psychology, 51,* 1173-1182.

Bates, J. E., Maslin, C. A., & Frankel, K. A. (1985). Attachment security, mother-child interaction, and temperament as predictors of behavior problem ratings at age three years. *Society for Research in Child Development Monographs, Special Issue, Growing Points in Attachment Theory and Research. (Serial no. 209), 50,* 167-193.

Baumrind, D. (1968). Authoritarian vs. authoritative parental control. *Adolescence, 3,* 255-272.

Baumrind, D. (1991). The influence of parenting style on adolescent competence and substance use. *Journal of Early Adolescence, 11,* 56-95.

Berger, K. S. (2005). *The developing person through the life span.* New York: Worth Publishers.

Bowlby, J. (1969). *Attachment.* New York: Basic Books.

Bowlby, J. (1982). *Attachment and loss: Vol. 1. Attachment (Second edition).* New York: Basic Books.

Bradley, R. H., & Corwyn, R. F. (2005). Caring for children around the world: A view from HOME. *International Journal of Behavioural Development, 29,* 468-478.

Bugental, D. B., Blue, J., & Cruzcosa, M. (1989). Perceived control over care giving outcomes: Implications for child abuse. *Developmental Psychology, 25,* 532-539.

Bugental, D. B., & Shennum, W. A. (1984). "Difficult" children as elicitors and targets of adult communication patterns: An attributional-behavioral transactional analysis. *Monographs of the Society for Research in Child Development, 49* (1, Serial No. 205), 1-69.

Buss, A. H., & Plomin, R. (1975). *A temperament theory of personality development.* New York: Wiley.

Calkins, S. D., Hungerford, A., & Dedmon, S. E. (2004). Mothers' interactions with temperamentally frustrated infants. *Infant Mental Health Journal, 25,* 219-239.

Carlson, E., & Sroufe, L. (1995). Contributions of attachment theory to developmental psychopathology. In D. Cicchetti & D. Cohen (Eds.), *Developmental psychopathology, Vol. 1: Theory and Methods* (pp. 581-617). Oxford, England: John Wiley & Sons.

Chang, L., Schwartz, D., Dodge, K., & McBride-Change, C. (2003). Harsh parenting in relation to child emotion regulation and aggression. *Journal of Family Psychology, 17,* 598-606.

Cole, P. M., Michel, M., & Teti, L. (1994). The development of emotion regulation and dysregulation: A clinical perspective. *Monographs of the Society for Research in Child Development, 59,* 73-100.

Collins, W. A., Maccoby, E. E., Steinberg, L., Hetherington, E. M., & Bornstein, M. H. (2000). Contemporary research on parenting: The case for nature and nurture. *American Psychologist, 55,* 218-232.

Deater-Deckard, K., & Dodge, K. (1997). Externalizing behavior problems and discipline revisited: Nonlinear effects and variation by culture, context, and gender. *Psychological Inquiry, 8,* 161-175.

DeGangi, G. A. (2000). *Pediatric disorders of regulation in affect and behavior: A therapists guide to assessment and treatment (Practical resources for the mental health professional).* San Diego, CA: Academic Press.

Dix, T., & Grusec, J. (1985). Parental attributional processes in the socialization of children. In I. Siegel (Ed.), *Parental belief systems: The psychological consequences for children* (pp. 201-223). Hillside, NJ: Lawrence Erlbaum.

Dix, T., & Lochman, J. (1990). Social cognitions and negative reactions to children: A comparison of mothers of aggressive and nonaggressive boys. *Journal of Social and Clinical Psychology, 9,* 418-438.

Dix, T., Ruble, D., Grusec, J., & Nixon, S. (1986). Social cognition in parents: Inferential and affective reactions to children of three age levels. *Child Development, 57,* 879-894.

Eisenberg, N., Fabes, R., Shepard, S., Guthrie, I., Murphy, B., & Reiser, M. (1999). Parental reactions to children's negative emotions: Longitudinal relations to quality of children's social functioning. *Child Development, 70,* 513-534.

Fiske, S. T., & Taylor, S. E. (1984). *Social cognition.* New York: Random House.

Ge, X., Conger, R. D., & Elder, G. H. (1996). Coming of age too early: Pubertal influences on girls' vulnerability to psychological distress. *Child Development, 67,* 3386-3400.

Gerard, A. (1994). *Parent-Child Relationship Inventory (PCRI): Manual.* Los Angeles, CA: Western Psychological Services.

Goldsmith, H. H., Buss, A. H., Plomin, R., Rothbart, T. A., Chess, S., Hinde, R. A., et al. (1987). Round table. What is temperament? Four approaches. *Child Development, 58,* 505-529.

Greenspan, S. I. (2007). Levels of infant-caregiver interactions and the DIR model: Implications for the development of signal affects, the regulation of mood and behavior, the formation of a sense of self, the creation of internal representation, and the construction of defenses and character structure. *Journal of Infant, Child, and Adolescent Psychotherapy, 6,* 174-210.

Hayes, S. C., & Ju, W. (1995). The applied implications of rule-governed behavior. In W. O'Donohue & L. Krasner (Eds.), *Theories of behavior therapy: Exploring behavior change* (pp. 374-391). Washington, DC: American Psychological Association.

Heider, F. (1958). *The psychology of interpersonal relations.* New York: Wiley.

Hollingshead, A. B. (1975). *Four factor index of social status.* Yale University: Unpublished manuscript.

Jennings, K. D. (2004). Development of goal-directed behaviour and related self-processes in toddlers. *International Journal of Behavioral Development, 28,* 319-327.

Kagan, J. (2003). Biology, context, and developmental inquiry. *Annual Review of Psychology, 54,* 1-23.

Keenan, K., & Shaw, D. (1995). The development of coercive family processes: The interaction between aversive toddler behavior and parenting factors. In J. McCord (Ed.), *Coercion and punishment in long-term perspectives* (pp. 165-180). New York: Cambridge University Press.

Kochanska, G., & Knaack, A. (2003). Effortful control as a personality characteristic of young children: Antecedents, correlates, and consequences. *Journal of Personality, 71,* 1087-1112.

NICHD Early Child Care Research Network. (2004). Affect dysregulation in the mother-child relationship in the toddler years: Antecedents and consequences. *Development and Psychopathology, 16,* 43-68.

O'Connor, T. G. (2002). Annotation: The 'effects' of parenting reconsidered: Findings, challenges, and applications. *Journal of Child Psychology and Psychiatry, 43,* 555-572.

O'Connor, T. G., Deater Deckard, K., Fulker, D., Rutter, M., & Plomin, R. (1998). Genotype-environment correlations in late childhood and early adolescence: Antisocial behavioral problems and coercive parenting. *Developmental Psychology, 34,* 970-981.

Patterson, G. R. (1982). *Coercive family process.* Eugene, OR: Castalia.

Patterson, G. R., DeBaryshe, B. D., & Ramsey, E. (1989). A developmental perspective on antisocial behavior. *American Psychologist, 44,* 329-335.

Phares, V., & Renk, K. (1998). Perception of parents: A measure of adolescents' feelings about their parents. *Journal of Marriage and Family, 60,* 646-659.

Putnam, S. P., & Rothbart, M. K. (2006). Development of short and very short forms of the Children's Behavior Questionnaire. *Journal of Personality Assessment, 87,* 102-112.

Renk, K. (in press). Mothers' perceptions of young children, parenting, and young children's behavior problems. *Child and Family Behavior Therapy.*

Renk, K., Klein, J., Oliveros, A., & McKinney, C. (2006). The parent-young child relationship: Dealing with and surviving toddlerhood. In D. Devore (Ed.), *Parent-child relationships: New research* (pp. 83-99). Hauppauge, NY: Nova Science Publishers, Inc.

Renk, K., Lauer, B., Weaver, R., Scott, S. L., Middleton, M., & White, R. (in press). Effortful control: Linkages to regulation disorders and attention-deficit/hyperactivity disorder. In A. M. Columbus (Ed.), *Advances in psychology research* (Vol. 72). Hauppage, NY: Nova Science Publishers, Inc.

Renk, K., Roddenberry, A., Oliveros, A., & Sieger, K. (2007). The relationship of maternal characteristics and perceptions of children to children's emotional and behavioral problems. *Child and Family Behavior Therapy, 29,* 37-57.

Rothbart, M. K., Ahadi, S. A., Hershey, K. L., & Fisher, P. (2001). Investigations of temperament at three to seven years: The Children's Behavior Questionnaire. *Child Development, 72,* 1394-1408.

Rothbart, M. K., & Bates, J. E. (2006). Temperament. In N. Eisenberg (Ed.), *Handbook of child psychology: Vol. 3. Social, emotional, and personality development (6th ed.,* pp. 99-166). New York: Wiley.

Rubin, K. H., Burgess, K. B., Dwyer, K. M., & Hastings, P. D. (2003). Predicting preschoolers' externalizing behaviors from toddler temperament, conflict, and maternal negativity. *Developmental Psychology, 39,* 164-176.

Scaramella, L.V., & Leve, L. D. (2004). Clarifying parent-child reciprocities during early childhood: The Early Childhood Coercion Model. *Clinical Child and Family Psychology Review, 7,* 89-107.

Shaw, D. S., Owens, E. B., Giovannelli, J., & Winslow, E. B. (2001). Infant and toddler pathways leading to early externalizing disorders. *Journal of the American Academy of Child and Adolescent Psychiatry, 40,* 36-43.

Shaw, D. S., Winslow, E. B., Ownes, E. B., Vondra, J. I., Cohn, J. F., & Bell, R. Q. (1998). The development of early externalizing problems among children from low-income families: A transformational perspective. *Journal of Abnormal Child Psychology, 26,* 95-107.

Snyder, J., Cramer, A., Afrank, J., & Patterson, G. R. (2005). The contribution of ineffective discipline and parental hostile attributions of child misbehavior to the development of conduct problems at home and school. *Developmental Psychology, 41,* 30-41.

Spinrad, T. L., Eisenberg, N., Gaertner, B., Popp, T., Smith, C. L., Kupfer, A., et al. (2007). Relations of maternal socialization and toddlers' effortful control to children's adjustment and social competence. *Developmental Psychology, 43,* 1170-1186.

Strassberg, Z. (1995). Social information processing in compliance situations by mothers of behavior-problem boys. *Child Development, 66,* 376-389.

Thomas, A., & Chess, S. (1977). *Temperament and development.* New York: Brunner/Mazel.

Thomas, A., Chess, S., & Birch, H. G. (1968). *Temperament and behavior disorders in children.* New York: New York University Press.

Thomas, A., Chess, S., Birch, H. G., Hertzig, M. E., & Korn, S. (1963). *Behavioural individuality in early childhood.* New York: New York University Press.

Webster-Stratton, C., & Eyberg, S. (1982). Child temperament: Relationship with child behavior problems and parent-child interactions. *Journal of Clinical Child Psychology, 11,* 123-129.

Author Note

This manuscript is based on the Honors Thesis of the first author under the direction of the second author. Special thanks to Valerie K. Sims, Ph.D., and John Manning, Ed.D., for their comments on an earlier version of this manuscript. Also, special thanks to Marcia Diebler and the staff at the Creative School for their willingness to work with us.

Maternal Attributional Style and Infant Attachment

Janice H. Kennedy
Georgia Southern University

Maternal characteristics associated with mother-infant attachment security are of interest to both attachment researchers and to clinicians. In the current study, the relations among mother-infant attachment, emotional expressivity, and maternal attributional style were examined. Seventy-two mother-infant pairs were videotaped in the Strange Situation Procedure (SSP). Mothers then completed the Attributional Style Questionnaire and Self-expressiveness in the Family Questionnaire. Mothers of insecure-avoidant infants were more likely to make internal attributions for positive events than were mothers of secure or insecure-resistant infants. Maternal positive emotional expressivity was positively related to security of infant attachment. Thus, maternal attributional style and low positive emotional expressivity were seen as potential risk factors for the development of insecure attachment.

In Mary Ainsworth's (Ainsworth et al., 1978) seminal examination of maternal factors that shape the development of the caregiver-infant attachment relationship, maternal sensitivity, responsiveness, and appropriately stimulating play were associated with security of attachment. Mothers characterized as clinically depressed have been consistently reported to be low or inconsistent in these characteristics (e.g., Campbell et al., 2004; Martins & Gaffan, 2000; Teti, Gelfand, Messinger, & Isabella, 1995). Evidence suggests that one mechanism for the relationship between maternal depression and infant attachment may be via the mother's attributional style, or how one generally perceives control of positive and negative events in one's life (Peterson et al., 1982). Although individuals diagnosed with clinical depression typically present with a pessimistic attributional style (perceiving little or no control over events in their lives, or perhaps feeling responsible for primarily negative events), it has been suggested that nondepressed individuals may show a similar attributional style as a precursor to depression or evidence of mild (nonclinical) depression (Peterson et al.). The purpose of the present study was to explore the relationship in a low-risk sample between the mother's attributional style and the quality of the

All correspondence should be addressed to Janice H. Kennedy, Professor of Psychology, Georgia Southern University, P. O. Box 8041, Statesboro, GA 30460. Electronic mail may be sent to: jkennedy@georgiasouthern.edu.

mother-infant attachment relationship to determine whether mothers perhaps prone to depressive thoughts and behaviors may be less likely to have secure attachment relationships with their infants.

First, an understanding of how maternal depression contributes to the quality of the attachment relationship is important. Maternal depression may influence infant functioning both directly and indirectly. As Egeland and Sroufe (1981) point out, a deviant childrearing environment, including possibly sad facial expression and flat or inconsistent affect in interaction with the child, parental maltreatment or neglect, and negative maternal attributions toward the child may all influence infant development. Even cognitive development may be affected. Kaplan, Bachorowski, and Zarlengo-Strouse (1999) found that child-directed speech produced by depressed mothers did not promote associative learning in young infants. Children of depressed parents are particularly likely to be faced with physical, or at least emotional, unavailability of parents, or unstable, ineffective interaction patterns for long, unpredictive periods of time (Cicchetti, Toth, & Rogosch, 1999). They are more frequently exposed to parental sadness and dysphoria, helplessness and hopelessness, and irritability and confusion than children of nondepressed parents (De Wolff & van IJzendoorn, 1997). Maternal depression has been associated with mothers' negative perceptions of (Barnett et al., 1999) and less engagement with (Campbell et al., 2004) their children. Mothers who are dysphoric have been reported to show less emotional expressivity as well with their infants (Halberstadt, Cassidy, Stifter, Parke, & Fox, 1995). In a large-scale NICHD Early Child Care Research Network study (1999), women with chronic symptoms of depression were less sensitive when observed playing with their children from infancy through 36 months than other mothers. Maternal insensitivity has been reported in samples showing a subjective feeling of helplessness in mothers (Spangler & Grossman, 1999). Even in prospective studies, a relation between maternal psychological unavailability (including separation or loss; Bowlby, 1980) and insecurity of attachment has been reported (Radke-Yarrow, 1991). Thus, the main constituents of sensitivity to infant bids for attention—promptness of response, consistency, and appropriateness (van den Boom, 1997)—are uncommon responses by depressed mothers.

Depressed individuals tend to have a negative view of the world, and this view may lead to a further propensity toward depression, as one feels more and more helpless in an uncontrollable world. The learned helplessness model (Peterson & Seligman, 1984; Peterson et al., 1982) proposes that depressive symptoms are associated with an explanatory style in which uncontrollable bad events are attributed to internal, stable, and global causes, while positive events are seen as external, unstable, and specific to a particular situation. The Attributional Style Questionnaire (Peterson et al.) measures the causal attributions for potential positive and negative personal events offered by individuals at risk for depression. One's attributional style for negative events can be predicted by early childhood, as well as influence later developmental outcome. Nolen-Hoeksema, Girgus, and Seligman (1992) found that a pessimistic explanatory style in childhood predicted adult depression.

In the developmental literature, parental attributions about ambiguous child intentions and behavior have been examined with regard to family stress and child characteristics. For example, Henderson, Cobb, and Horn (1997) reported that at-risk mothers' attributional ratings of ambiguously caused child misbehaviors were more negative than comparison mothers' ratings with regard to blame, anger, punishment, and behavioral severity. Parents of children with Conduct Disorder (CD) were more likely to regard their children's misbehavior as intentional and to attribute it to stable, global causes beyond the parents' control than were parents of children without CD. They were also less likely to see their own parenting as effective, perhaps leading to feelings of blame and helplessness that contribute to aversive parent behavior or parental withdrawal in child-parent conflict (Baden & Howe, 1992; Snyder, Cramer, Afrank, & Patterson, 2005). Child behavior may thus influence attributional style, and parents' attributional style may in turn influence parenting behaviors.

In the present study, however, maternal attributions are defined more broadly than relating specifically to child behavior (Corr & Gray, 1996; Peterson et al., 1982; Peterson & Seligman, 1984; Tennen & Herzberger, 1985). Attributional or explanatory) style as used here relates to events occurring across several domains in the mother's life: romantic relationships, employment success, physical attractiveness, friendship, etc. Events are judged as either due to one's own efforts or beyond one's control, the cause of the event is judged as stable or temporary, and the cause is judged as global or applicable only to that specific situation. This more general attributional style has been related to clinical depression and its precursors in clinical psychology (Peterson & Seligman).

Even in the absence of clinical depression recent evidence suggests that one mechanism for the relation between maternal insensitivity and infant attachment may be via maternal attributional style. For example, Barnett et al. (1999), in examining mother-infant relations in families with neurologically challenged infants, found that mothers with the most positive scores on the Positive Dysfunctional Attributions Scale were more likely to have children classified as disorganized in attachment. These parents appear to have taken on seemingly unrealistically positive views of their role as caregivers. The authors suggest that such unrealistic optimism may be a marker for less positive outcome for the child's development later on. When O'Connor (1997) examined *Minnesota Multiphasic Personality Inventory* (MMPI) responses of mothers with securely attached infants, she found that they scored higher than mothers of insecure infants on Psychopathic Deviance and lower on the Introversion Scale. Mothers of secure infants admitted to significantly more family problems and described themselves as less introverted than mothers of insecure infants. In contrast, mothers of insecure infants evidenced more denial and increased introversion. Others have found that caregivers of children categorized as disorganized in attachment report the lowest levels of stress in childrearing (Moss, Rousseau, Parent, St-Laurent, & Saintonge, 1998; Stevenson-Hinde & Shouldice, 1995). These findings suggest that mothers at risk for developing insecure relationships with their children may be unrealistic in their assessments of potential problems in the home and therefore unprepared to deal realistically with stressors in their lives.

Although the evidence seems clear that infants of clinically depressed mothers are at risk for problems in forming secure attachments with their infants, currently evidence is lacking as to whether one's general attributional style is predictive of mother-infant attachment security. The purpose of the present study was to explore the relation between mother-infant attachment and maternal attributional style (optimistic versus pessimistic/depressive). Research is needed that specifically examines whether a negative attributional style (that may be a precursor of depression) or an optimistic attributional style (which may be associated with denial and insensitivity) in mothers of young infants is related to mother-infant security of attachment.

Method

Participants

Participants were recruited from introductory psychology, family life, and education classes in a mid-sized university, as well as from the surrounding rural community. Seventy-two mothers ($M\ age$ = 28.22 years, SD = 9.50 years) and their infants (43 girls/29 boys; $M\ age$ = 14.91 months, SD = 3.59 months) participated in the study. Seventy-seven percent were Caucasian and 23% were African-American. Forty-two percent of the infants had 1-3 siblings (5% had a younger sibling). Eighty-four percent of the mothers had at least some college education, and all but one had finished high school. Sixty (84%) of the mothers were either employed at least part-time or were college students. The child's father resided in the home in 77% (n = 55) of the cases.

Measures

Ainsworth Strange Situation Procedure (SSP). This standardized procedure (Ainsworth et al., 1978) took place in a laboratory setting with two chairs for adults facing one another and about 7 feet apart. A child's chair with eight toys scattered around it was on the other side of the room perpendicular to the adult chairs and 8 feet away from them. Mothers were instructed to respond briefly and appropriately as they normally would to their infants' bids for interaction, but to try not to direct the infants' play or other behaviors. The SSP consists of a series of eight increasingly stressful 3-minute episodes for the infant. These episodes are:

1. Experimenter, Mother, Infant (uncoded)
2. Mother, Infant
3. Mother, Infant, Stranger
4. Infant, Stranger
5. Mother, Infant
6. Infant
7. Infant, Stranger
8. Mother, Infant

Thus, in this procedure, there are opportunities to observe the infant's exploration of the environment from a secure base, responses to an adult female stranger with the mother present and again when the mother is absent, and reunion with the mother after two brief separations. The entire 24-minute session was videotaped through a two-way mirror. The procedure's reliability and validity have been well documented (Ainsworth et al.).

Attributional Style Questionnaire (ASQ). This instrument (Peterson et al., 1982) describes 12 different hypothetical events, half positive and half negative. Participants are asked to read each hypothetical event and to then briefly describe the most probable cause of the event. Then the participant rates the cause on a 7-point Likert-type scale with regard to internality, stability, and globality. The ASQ yields total scores for internality, stability, and globality collapsed across the six hypothetical situations for both positive events and negative events. It also yields Composite scores for positive events (internal, global, and stability) and negative events, as well as an overall Optimism score (CPCN; Composite Positive minus Composite Negative Score). High scores for positive events reflect an optimistic outlook (positive events are viewed as due to internal, stable, and global causes), while high scores for negative events reflect a pessimistic or depressive outlook (negative events are viewed as due to internal, stable, and global causes; Tennen & Herzberger, 1985). Adequate internal consistency for the composite attributional style scales for good events and bad events (Cronbach's *alpha* coefficients of .75 and .72, respectively; Peterson et al.) was found. Test-retest reliability across a 5-week period was found to range between .57 and .70 (Peterson et al.) for each subtest. Evidence of adequate construct, predictive, and content validity has been demonstrated (Corr & Gray, 1996; Tennen & Herzberger).

Self-expressiveness in the Family Questionnaire (SEFQ). The SEFQ (Halberstadt et al., 1995) measures the frequency of an individual's emotional expression within a family context for common situations. Individuals completing the questionnaire are asked to rate 40 hypothetical scenarios on a 9-point scale with regard to expression of feelings in a particular situation. There are two subscales: positive emotion and negative emotion.

Internal consistency (Cronbach's *alpha*) of these scales has been reported to be .87 - .94 across four studies for the positive, negative, and total scales.

Test-retest reliability has been stable over periods as long as one year. Convergent, discriminant, and construct validity also appear to be adequate (Haberstadt et al., 1995).

Procedure

After the experimental procedure was explained to the mothers, they signed an informed consent form and retained a copy for their records. When the procedure began, mothers and infants were videotaped through a one-way mirror in an experimental playroom modeled after Ainsworth's strange situation room (Ainsworth et al., 1978). There were chairs for the mother and the stranger, and a child's chair surrounded by toys about 8 feet away from the adult chairs. A female graduate student experienced with young children served as the adult female stranger. After the Strange Situation Procedure, mothers completed the ASQ and the SEFQ, along with demographic information.

Reliability Measures and Data Analysis

The SSP videotapes were coded by three formally trained coders (the author and two graduate students) blind to other information about the mother and child. All 72 assessments were coded using the standard attachment classifications of secure, insecure-avoidant, anxious-resistant, and disorganized (Ainsworth et al., 1978; Main & Hesse, 1990). When coders disagreed, a classification was assigned by consensus. Average agreement with the 4-category classification system was .84 ($\kappa = .70$). Forty-five securely attached infants, 10 insecure-avoidant infants, 9 insecure-resistant infants, and 8 disorganized infants were identified in the sample.

Two overall multivariate analyses of variance (MANOVAs) were conducted to determine whether infant attachment classification was related to maternal attributional style and to maternal expressivity. When significant results were found, individual analyses of variance (ANOVAs) were conducted to determine specific relationships.

Results

Infant Attachment Classifications and Maternal Attributional Style

One-way ANOVAs were conducted to determine whether infant attachment classification (secure, insecure-avoidant, insecure-resistant, or disorganized) was related to internal, stable, or global attributions for positive and negative events (see Table 1). Post-hoc analyses using Tukey's HSD tests showed that mothers of insecure-avoidant or disorganized infants were significantly more likely to interpret positive events as being due to their own efforts (internal attributions) than were mothers of secure or insecure-resistant infants. However, only mothers of avoidant infants were significantly more likely to interpret positive events as

Table 1

Means and Standard Deviations for Maternal Attributional Style by Infant Attachment Classification

	Infant Classification					
	Secure	Avoidant	Resistant	Disorganized		
ASQ	M	M	M	M	F	p
Positive Events						
Internal	4.74_a (.67)	5.40_b (.92)	4.28_a (.71)	5.16_b (.62)	4.711	.013*
Stable	5.00_a (.61)	5.37_a (1.05)	4.86_a (.38)	5.06_a (.63)	1.217	.324
Global	5.21_a,b (.76)	5.80_b (.82)	5.35_a,b (.85)	4.62_a (1.15)	3.236	.027*
Negative Events						
Internal	4.23_a (.72)	3.91_a (.95)	4.27_a (.51)	4.19_a (.68)	.121	.912
Stable	4.04_a (.71)	4.15_a (.63)	4.31_a (.51)	4.44_a (.79)	.38	.681
Global	3.99_a (.67)	3.76_a (1.42)	4.25_a (.67)	4.14_a (1.14)	.483	.594
CPCN	3.02_a (2.26)	4.42_b (3.73)	2.99_a (2.58)	2.09_a (3.66)	4.708	.018*

Note. ASQ = Attributional Style Questionnaire; CPCN = Composite Attributional Style Scores

Standard Deviations are given in parentheses.

Means sharing a common subscript do not differ significantly from one another

*p < .05

global (affecting other areas of their lives), compared to mothers of disorganized infants. With regard to Composite Attributional Style Scores (CPCN), mothers of avoidant infants scored significantly higher than did mothers of secure, insecure-resistant and disorganized infants.

Maternal Emotional Expressivity Ratings and Infant Attachment Classification

There was a relation between maternal ratings of positive emotional expressivity in the home and infant attachment classification. A one-way ANOVA revealed that infant attachment classification was related to maternal ratings of positive expression of emotion in the child's home, $F(2,47) = 3.68$, $p = .04$.

Post-hoc analyses revealed that mothers of secure infants reported higher positive emotional expression (M = 187.46) than mothers of resistant and disorganized infants (Ms = 139.40 and 141.28, respectively). Positive emotional expression scores of mothers of secure infants did not differ from those of mothers of avoidant infants (M = 155.67). There was no relation between reported maternal negative emotional expression in the home and infant attachment classification.

An unexpected post-hoc finding was that when the father resided in the child's home, mothers reported higher positive emotional expressivity, $t(48)$ = 3.86, p = .04 (Ms = 170.00 and 153.94, respectively).

Discussion

Mothers of insecure-avoidant infants showed higher scores for internal attributions for positive events and an overall more optimistic attributional style than mothers of infants of other classifications. In light of the large body of literature illustrating the consistently positive correlates of security of attachment (e.g., Sroufe, 2005; Sroufe & Waters, 1977); one might expect that an optimistic outlook would be associated with a secure mother-infant relationship, as optimism is generally associated with a sense of internal control (Peterson & Seligman, 1984). However, in the present study mothers of insecure-avoidant infants appeared to be unrealistically optimistic about their own impact on positive events in their lives (attributing more control for themselves for positive events than mothers of infants in other classifications). With regard to caregiving, these mothers may attribute positive infant behaviors to their own parenting, but attribute negative infant behaviors to events beyond their control or as not worthy of their attention and efforts, resulting in less sensitivity to their infants' emotional needs.

Although mothers' attachment style was not assessed with the Adult Attachment Interview (Hesse, 2008), evidence from other studies suggest that the maternal responses of avoidant infants were consistent with a dismissing attachment style (Beherns, Hesse, & Main, 2007). For example, Pianta, Egeland, and Adam (1996) reported that dismissing (avoidant) mothers on the Adult Attachment Interview endorsed the lowest levels of anxiety-type symptoms on the MMPI-2. The authors suggest that these mothers were suppressing emotion and providing self-descriptions consistent with a view of the self as strong and independent. Similarly, others have reported that mothers of insecurely attached infants showed more denial and reported fewer problems in their families than mothers of secure infants (O'Connor, 1997) and were overly controlling (Donovan & Leavitt, 1989). With regard to disorganized attachment, Jacobsen and Miller (1999) found that mothers whose children were classified as disorganized were the most prone to have skewed and particularly glorified representations of their children. These findings suggest that a pessimistic attributional style may be less predictive for mothers of insecure infants than expected, and an unrealistically optimistic attributional style more predictive. Bretherton (2005) explains Bowlby's view of defensive strategies that protect one from awareness of available, but potentially anxiety-provoking, information. When an individual has developed two inconsistent working models of the same relationship, only one is dominant in consciousness while the other is repressed. Attribution-making, representational processes and views not only reflect reality, but they create different realities for self and relationship partners. Thus, mothers of avoidant and disorganized infants may have unrealistic views about their infants and themselves, and this may contribute to insensitivity in parenting.

Maternal family emotional expressivity was also related to infant attachment classification. Mothers of secure infants reported higher positive emotional expressiveness. There was no difference among mothers according to infant attachment classification for the expression of negative emotion. However, mothers reported greater positive emotional expressivity when the father was present in the home. The role of the father's presence as a modifier of relations between maternal emotional expressivity and attachment classification in the Strange Situation emphasizes the importance of the father's role in socioemotional development. Solomon and George (1999) found, likewise, that in separated/divorced families, repeated overnight separations from the primary caregiver were associated with insecure attachment to the mother. These findings underscore the importance of the father both directly and indirectly in supporting optimal infant development (Cowan, 1997).

There are potential limitations in the design of the present study. Of course, since this is a correlational study in design, caution must be displayed in describing the relationship between attributional style and infant attachment classification, since we cannot determine the contribution of third variables such as marital conflict or other stressors that may contribute to both the development of an insecure attachment relationship and to mothers' attributional style. Other limitations to design can be addressed in future studies. For example, even a short-term longitudinal study in which mothers' attributional style is measured at several points in time instead of only one would provide more confidence than the present single measure as a stable trait. Moreover, since insecure and disorganized attachment classifications appear less frequently in the general population than secure classifications, a larger sample would provide greater numbers of infants in these insecure categories, leading to more power in differentiating among them.

There are other avenues to be addressed in future research as well. First, if mothers' dysphoric mood states and/or depression affect one's parenting, does it matter if the mood state is chronic or episodic? If episodic, is depression in one period of development more important than another? A maternal depressed mood may be particularly problematic as infants approach the end of their first year (Belsky, Rosenberger, & Crnic, 1995). Mothers who feel significant stress and depression may be unprepared to handle behaviors that result from their toddler's developing insistence on autonomy (Goodman & Gotlib, 1999). Second, what is the effect of having two parents with depression or a negative attributional style? It can be assumed that having one nondepressed but involved parent may somewhat ameliorate the effects of the other parent's depression, but this potential protective effect has not been examined adequately. Cohn, Campbell, and Ross (1991) reported that infants of depressed mothers were less likely to be insecurely attached when cared for during their first year in nonmaternal care than when cared for primarily by their depressed mothers. Depression and attributional style need to be examined in both mothers and fathers.

In conclusion, an unrealistically optimistic maternal attributional style may reflect insensitivity to infant social and emotional needs, culminating in an insecure attachment relationship. These findings underscore the need for prevention and for early identification and treatment of depression. They also suggest intervention strategies to provide support for mothers at risk for developing insensitive and inappropriate interaction patterns with their infants. For example, Lieberman, Padron, van Horn, and Harris (2005), working with inseure mother-infant dyads, demonstrated the benefits of promoting mothers' positive, coherent maternal representations of their insecurely attached infants. Such strategies may involve parent sensitivity training and relationship enhancement programs, especially those that focus on social information processing (e.g., Bosquet & Egeland, 2001; Brestan, Eyberg, Boggs, & Algina, 1997; Schuhmann, Foote, Eyberg, Boggs, & Algina, 1998). Specifically, Moss, Cyr and Dubois-Comtois (2004) have proposed intervention directed at correcting the disparity between mothers' internal working models of caregiving and the child's actual needs. Certainly the mothers of insecure-avoidant and disorganized infants in the current sample appeared to have unrealistic views about their infants and themselves, which may contribute to insensitivity in parenting. Challenging faulty perceptions of infant behavior and needs and increasing the repertoire of mothers' positive responses in interactions with their infants would enhance the opportunities to form a secure attachment.

References

Ainsworth, M. D. S., Blehar, M. C., Waters, E. C., & Wall, S. N. (1978). *Patterns of attachment: A psychological study of the strange situation.* Hillsdale, NJ: Lawrence Erlbaum Associates.

Baden, A. D., & Howe, G. W. (1992). Mothers' attributions and expectancies regarding their conduct-disordered children. *Journal of Abnormal Child Psychology, 20,* 467-485.

Barnett, D., Hunt, K. H., Butler, C. M., McCaskill, J. W., IV, Kaplan-Estrin, M., & Pipp-Siegel, S. (1999). Indices of disorganized attachment among toddlers with neurological and non-neurological problems. In J. Solomon & C. George (Eds.), *Attachment disorganization* (pp. 189-212). New York: Guilford.

Beherns, K. Y., Hesse, E., & Main, M. (2007). Mothers' attachment status as determined by the Adult Attachment Interview predicts their 6-year-old's reunion responses: A study conducted in Japan. *Developmental Psychology, 43,* 1553-1567.

Belsky, J., Rosenberger, K., & Crnic, K. (1995). The origins of attachment security: "Classical" and contextual determinants. In S. Goldberg, R. Muir, & J. Kerr (Eds.), *Attachment theory: Social, developmental, and clinical perspectives* (pp. 153-183). Hillsdale, NJ: Analytic Press.

Bowlby, J. (1980). *Attachment and Loss. Vol. 3. Separation.* London: Basic Books.

Bosquet, M., & Egeland, B. (2001). Associations among maternal depressive symptomatology, state of mind and parent and child behaviors: Implications for attachment-based interventions. *Attachment & Human Development, 3,* 173-199.

Brestan, E. V., Eyberg, S. M., Boggs, S .R., & Algina, J. (1997). Parent-child interaction therapy: Parents' perceptions of untreated siblings. *Child & Family Behavior Therapy, 19,* 13-28.

Bretherton, I. (2005). In pursuit of the internal working model construct and its relevance to attachment relationships. In K. E. Grossman, K. Grossman, & E. Waters (Eds.), *Attachment from infancy to adulthood: The major longitudinal studies* (pp. 13-47). New York: Guilford Press.

Campbell, S. B., Brownell, C. A., Hungerford, A., Spieker, S. J., Mohan, R., & Blessing, J. S. (2004). The course of maternal depressive symptoms and maternal sensitivity as predictors of attachment security at 36 months. *Development and Psychopathology, 16,* 231-252.

Cicchetti, D., Toth, S. L., & Rogosch, F. A. (1999). The efficacy of toddler-parent psychotherapy to increase attachment security in offspring of depressed mothers. *Attachment & Human Development, 1,* 34-66.

Cohn, J., Campbell, S., & Ross, S. (1991). Infant response in the still face paradigm at 6 months predicts avoidant and secure attachment at 12 months. *Development & Psychopathology, 3*, 367-376.

Corr, P. J., & Gray, J. A. (1996). Structure and validity of the Attributional Style Questionnaire: A cross-sample comparison. *The Journal of Psychology, 130*, 645-657.

Cowan, P. A. (1997). Beyond meta-analysis: A plea for a family systems view of attachment. *Child Development, 68*, 601-603.

De Wolff, M. S., & van IJzendoorn, M. H. (1997). Sensitivity and attachment: A meta-analysis on parental antecedents of infant attachment. *Child Development, 68*, 571-591.

Donovan, W. L., & Leavitt, L. A. (1989). Maternal self-efficacy and infant attachment: Integrating physiology, perceptions, and behavior. *Child Development, 60*, 460-472.

Egeland, B., & Sroufe, L. A. (1981). Development sequelae of maltreatment in infancy. *New Directions for Child Development, 11*, 77-92.

Goodman, S. H., & Gotlib, I. H. (1999). Risk for psychopathology in the children of depressed mothers: A developmental model for understanding mechanisms of transmissions. *Psychological Review, 106*, 458-490.

Halberstadt, A. G., Cassidy, J., Stifter, C. A., Parke, R. D., & Fox, N. A. (1995). Self-expressiveness within the family context: Psychometric support for a new measure. *Psychological Assessment, 7*, 93-103.

Henderson, T. B., Cobb, M. J., & Horn, M. (1997, April). *Attributions for child misbehaviors among African-American at-risk mothers.* Paper presented at the biennial meeting of the Society for Research in Child Development, Washington, D.C.

Hesse, E. (2008). The Adult Attachment Interview. In J. Cassidy & P. R. Shaver (Eds.), *Handbook of attachment: Theory, research and clinical application* (2nd ed., pp. 552-598). New York: Guilford Press.

Jacobsen, T., & Miller, L. J. (1999). Attachment quality in young children of mentally ill mothers: Contributions of maternal caregiving abilities and foster care context. In J. Solomon & C. George (Eds.), *Attachment disorganization.* (pp. 347-378). New York: Guilford.

Kaplan, P. S., Bachorowski, J., & Zarlengo-Strouse, P. (1999). Child-directed speech produced by mothers with symptoms of depression fails to promote associative learning in 4-month-old infants. *Child Development, 70*, 560-570.

Lieberman, A. F., Padron, E., van Horn, P, & Harris, W. (2005). Angels in the nursery: The intergenerational transmission of benevolent parental influences. *Infant Mental Health, 26*, 504-520.

Main, M., & Hesse, E. (1990). Parents' unresolved traumatic experiences are related to infant disorganized attachment status: Is frightened and/or frightening parental behavior the linking mechanism? In M. T. Greenberg, D. Cicchetti, & E. M. Cummings (Eds.), *Attachment in the preschool years: Theory, research, and intervention* (pp. 161-182). Chicago: University of Chicago Press.

Martins, C., & Gaffan, E. A. (2000). Effects of early maternal depression on patterns of infant-mother attachment: A meta-analytic investigation. *Journal of Child Psychology and Psychiatry, 41, 737-746.*

Moss, E., Cyr, C., & Dubois-Comtois, K. (2004). Attachment at early school age and developmental risk: Examining family contexts and behavior problems of controlling-caregiving, controlling-punitive and behaviorally disorganized children. *Developmental Psychology, 40,* 519-532.

Moss, E., Rousseau, D., Parent, S., St-Laurent, D., & Saintonge, J. (1998). Correlates of attachment at school age: Maternal reported stress, mother-child and behavior problems. *Child Development, 69,* 1390-1405.

NICHD Early Child Care Research Network. (1999). Chronicity of maternal depressive symptoms, maternal sensitivity, and child functioning at 36 months. *Developmental Psychology, 35,* 1297-1310.

Nolen-Hoeksema, S., Girgus, J. S., & Seligman, M. E. P. (1992). Predictors and consequences of childhood depressive symptoms: A 5-year longitudinal study. *Journal of Abnormal Psychology, 101,* 405-422.

O'Connor, M. J. (1997, April). *Maternal personality characteristics on the MMPI and infant attachment.* Paper presented at the biennial meeting of the Society for Research in Child Development, Washington, D. C.

Peterson, C., & Seligman, M. E. P. (1984). Causal explanations as a risk factor for depression: Theory and evidence. *Psychological Review, 91,* 347-374.

Peterson, C., Semmel, A., von Baeyer, C., Abramson, L. Y., Metalsky, G. I., & Seligman, M. E. P. (1982). The Attributional Style Questionnaire. *Cognitive Therapy and Research, 6,* 287-299.

Pianta, R. C., Egeland, B., & Adam, E. (1996). Adult attachment classification and self-reported psychiatric symptomatology as assessed by the MMPI-2. *Journal of Consulting and Clinical Psychology, 64,* 273- 281.

Radke-Yarrow, M. (1991). Attachment patterns in children of depressed mothers. In C. M. Parkes, J. Stevenson-Hinde, & P. Marris (Eds.), *Attachment across the life cycle* (pp. 115-126). New York: Routledge.

Schuhmann, E. M., Foote, R. C., Eyberg, S. M., Boggs, S. R., & Algina, J. (1998). Efficacy of parent-child interaction therapy: Interim report of a randomized trial with short-term maintenance. *Journal of Clinical Child Psychology, 27, 34-45.*

Snyder, J., Cramer, A., Afrank, J., & Patterson, G. R. (2005). The contributions of ineffective discipline and parental hostile attributions of child misbehavior to the development of conduct problems at home and school. *Developmental Psychology, 41*, 30-41.

Solomon, J., & George, C. (1999). The effects on attachment of overnight visitation in divorced and separated families: A longitudinal follow-up. In J. Solomon & C. George (Eds.), *Attachment disorganization* (pp. 243-264). New York: Guilford.

Spangler, G., & Grossmann, K. (1999). Individual and physiological correlates of attachment disorganization in infancy. In J. Solomon & C. George (Eds.), *Attachment disorganization* (pp. 95-124). New York: Guilford.

Sroufe, L. A. (2005). Attachment and development: A prospective, longitudinal study from birth to adulthood. *Attachment & Human Development, 7*, 349-367.

Sroufe, L. A., & Waters, E. (1977). Attachment as an organizational construct. *Child Development, 48*, 1184-1199.

Stevenson-Hinde, J., & Shouldice, A. (1995). Maternal interactions and self-reports related to attachment classification at 4.5 years. *Child Development, 66*, 583-596.

Tennen, H., & Herzberger, S. (1985). Attributional Style Questionnaire. In D. J. Keyser & R. C. Sweetland (Eds.), *Test critiques*. (Vol. 4, pp. 20-30). Kansas City: Test Corporation of America.

Teti, D. M., Gelfand, D. M., Messinger, D. S., & Isabella, R. (1995). Maternal depression and the quality of early attachment: An examination of infants, preschoolers, and their mothers. *Developmental Psychology, 31*, 364-376.

van den Boom, D. C. (1997). Sensitivity and attachment: Next steps for developmentalists. *Child Development, 68*, 592-597.

Author Note

The author would like to thank Shauna Wilson, Lauren Beam, Lyndsay Itoh, Heather Lindsey, and Forrest Rackham for assistance in conducting this study, as well as the mothers and infants who gave so freely of their time to participate.

Current Measures for Assessing Parenting of Young Children

Barbara A. Mowder, Renee Shamah, & Taoxin Zeng
Pace University

This article primarily reviews current assessment measures for assessing the parenting of young children. Although there is significant research linking parenting with numerous child outcome variables, there are relatively few psychometrically and theoretically strong parent assessment measures. Parenting may be considered in terms of parent behaviors, children's needs, parent-child relationships, family dynamics, and the social-cultural milieu. Focusing on parent behaviors and parent-child relationships, this article highlights a number of measures which are pertinent to clinical and research use. In addition, some contemporary parent education programs are discussed briefly.

Research links parenting with a host of child outcome variables, such as academic achievement (Collins, Maccoby, Steinberg, Hetherington, & Bornstein, 2000), cognitive development (Ryan, Martin, & Brooks-Gunn, 2006), dropping out of school (Marcus & Sanders-Reio, 2001), and emotional regulation (Dallaire et al., 2006). Further, parenting is related to children's social-emotional development in terms of misbehavior (DelVecchio & O'Leary, 2006), social-emotional adjustment (Brook, Zheng, Whiteman, & Brook, 2001), and social skills (Rhoades & O'Leary, 2007). Although these linkages are firmly presented in the research literature, there seems to be relatively little interest in assessing parenting in school and clinical settings. Yet, parent assessment, as well as parent education, is critical in order to address to the needs of children and their families. In assessing children, practitioners can focus not only on the individual child but take a broader perspective, capturing children's individual strengths and needs as well as the child's family dynamics and environmental milieu.

In contrast to child cognitive and social-emotional assessment instruments (e.g., *Wechsler Intelligence Scale for Children-Fourth Edition, Behavior Assessment System for Children-Second Edition*), there is no "gold standard" in terms of measures regarding parenting. Even so, there are many parenting measures that are currently being used although they vary along a number of dimensions. For example, some can be used in clinical practice (e.g., to identify dysfunctional parenting styles) and others were designed for research use. In

All correspondence should be addressed to Barbara A. Mowder, Ph.D., Pace University, 41 Park Row, New York, NY 10038. Electronic mail may be sent to: bmowder@pace.edu.

addition, the instruments vary according to what they assess, and although some measure parenting globally, others assess specific parenting behaviors (e.g., discipline). The target populations for assessment also differ, with some designed for parents of children from specific age groups and others specifically for mothers or fathers. Further, other factors are in play in that some parenting measures are developmentally sensitive, psychometrically strong, and/or based on theory and a definition of parenting.

This article examines current parenting self-report measures rather than parent observation systems or interview protocols. Self-report measures tend to be easy to administer, user friendly, and cost-effective. Although observations have the advantage of providing direct indications of parenting behaviors, self-report measures offer the benefit of not being situation-specific. In the end, self-report measures tend to be practical and offer clinicians significant information for diagnostic, case conceptualization, and intervention purposes. In terms of this review, three measures of parent behaviors (i.e., *Parent Behavior Inventory, Parent Behavior Checklist, Parent Behavior Importance Questionnaire-Revised*) and two instruments regarding the parenting relationship (*Parent Child Relationship Inventory, Parent Relationship Questionnaire*) are examined in terms of:

1. Focus and purpose

2. Age of the child in relation to parenting

3. Scores obtained

4. Theoretical support

5. Evidence-based support and psychometric strength

6. Potential for intervention.

Parent Behavior Measures

Parent Behavior Inventory (PBI)

Lovejoy, Weis, O'Hare, and Rubin (1999) recognized that in dysfunctional families, parenting practices were often impaired in the areas of support/ engagement (e.g., behavior showing parents' acceptance through affection, shared activities, and support) and hostility/coercion (e.g., behavior expressing parents' negative feelings or indifference through coercion, threats, or physical punishment). The authors developed the *Parent Behavior Inventory* (PBI) to measure these dimensions in parents of young children, specifically preschool and young school-age children. Thus, the purpose of the PBI is to measure supportive/ engaged and hostile/coercive behaviors; the authors provide no specific theoretical basis for this scale. This measure, beyond serving as a self-report opportunity, may also be employed as an other-report (e.g., spouse, counselor) as well as an observational rating scale. The PBI can be used by researchers and clinicians under controlled conditions. That is, researchers can use the PBI to rate the parent's behaviors while the parent and child are in the low-stress (play) condition and the high-stress (task) condition. The flexibility in choice of respondents allows for the ability to circumvent many of the limitations (e.g., social desirability) associated with other self-report measures.

The PBI consists of 20 items or statements which are rated as "0" not at all true (I do not do this) through "5" very true (I often do this)(Lovejoy et al., 1999). Sample items include "I grab or handle my child roughly" (hostility/coercion item) and "I listen to my child's feelings and try to understand them" (support/engagement item). Factor analysis supports the PBI's two-factor structure, and reliability estimates were strong with an *alpha* coefficient of .81 for the hostile/coercive scale and .83 for the supportive/engaged scale (Lovejoy et al.). This measure also demonstrated strong test-retest reliability. In terms of validity, children's behavioral problems were positively correlated with the hostility/coercion scale, and negatively correlated with the support/engagement scale. This measure has the distinct advantage of providing a multi-informant, multi-situational measure of parenting and may also serve as part of a number of measures used to track family progress.

Parent Behavior Checklist (PBC)

The *Parent Behavior Checklist* (PBC) was developed by Fox (1994) to assess a family's strengths and needs. Fox identified three aspects of parenting including expectations (i.e., a parents developmental expectations such as "my child should use the toilet without help"), discipline (i.e., how a parent responds to difficult child behaviors), and nurturing (i.e., strategies parents use to promote their child's psychological growth). The PBC is unique in that it is based on a definition of parenting that states, "parenting is a dynamic process that includes the unique behaviors of a parent that a child directly experiences and that significantly impact his or her development. Parenting also includes parental expectations which children indirectly experience through their parents' behaviors" (Fox, 1994, p. 3). The PBC is based on a theoretical framework, specifically a developmental-environmental framework, which recognizes that a child's development results from an interaction between one's physical makeup and unique environmental experiences. In terms of environmental experiences, parental expectations and parental behaviors are viewed as paramount.

The PBC is a self-report measure that consists of 100 behaviors to which parents indicate frequency of behavioral performance using the scale of "1" almost never/never to "4" almost always/always (Fox, 1994). The PBC can be filled out by the mother, father, or primary caregiver though preliminary research done on this measure was conducted with mothers only. This measure is designed for use with parents of children 1 year through 4 years, 11 months of age, thus appreciating that parenting children of this age is different than parenting older children. Sample items for each of three subscales include, "My child should be old enough to share toys" for expectations, "I send my child to bed as a punishment" for discipline, and "I praise my child for learning new things" for nurturing.

The PBC has received extensive psychometric attention. Internal consistency findings for the three subscales are .97, .92, and .91, respectively, and test-retest results .98, .87, and .81. There were gender differences between mothers and fathers on the nurturing subscale, but not the other two subscales; the author attributes the gender differences as possibly due to scale development which occurred exclusively with mothers and not fathers (Fox, 1994).

Content validity was established through professional as well as parent review (Fox, 1994). Further, PBC subscale responses varied among parents with young children of different ages, and item to construct correlations were strong; each of these findings offer additional support for content validity. Concurrent validity was established by using the *Developmental Questionnaire* (DQ: Peters & Fox, 1993), convergent validity established by relating the PBC to the *Adult-Adolescent Parenting Inventory* (AAPI: Bavoleck, 1984), and discriminant validity was established by comparing PBC scores with responses to the *Child Behavior Checklist* (CBCL; Achenbach, 1991).

Parent Behavior Importance Questionnaire-Revised (PBIQ-R)

Mowder (2010) developed the *Parent Behavior Importance Questionnaire-Revised* (PBIQ-R) to measure perceptions of the importance of parenting behaviors. The measure is based on Mowder's parent development theory which defines parenting as the recognition, acceptance, and performance of the parenting role. The theory maintains that parenting beliefs develop over the life span, and parenting behaviors are generally consistent with those beliefs. Mowder's theory is developmentally sensitive and suggests that parent characteristics change in importance over time to accommodate children's developmental needs from infancy through adulthood. Based on previous research, Mowder established that there are six parent role characteristics including bonding, discipline, education, general welfare and protection, responsivity, and sensitivity (Mowder, 1994; Mowder, Harvey, Moy, & Pedro, 1995; Mowder, Harvey, Pedro, Rossen, & Moy, 1993); a negative factor was added later (Mowder, under review; Mowder & Shamah, in press). Unlike the other two parent measures (i.e., PBI, PBC) discussed, Mowder's measure focuses on a variety of positive parenting behaviors (e.g., bonding, education), instead of focusing mostly on those that are considered negative.

The PBIQ-R consists of 73 items representing six positive parenting subscales, as well as the seventh negative subscale (Mowder, 2010; Mowder & Shamah, 2010). The behaviors are rated as "0" not at all important to "4" extremely important. Examples of items include, "Smiling at your child" for bonding, "Talking with your child about rules" for discipline, "Reading to your child" for education, "Feeding, clothing, and sheltering your child" for general welfare and protection, "Answering your child's questions" for responsivity, and "Matching your responses to your child's needs" for sensitivity. An example of a negative item is "Yelling at your child." The overall PBIQ-R has a coefficient *alpha* of .96 and all of the subscales, with the exception of discipline, have *alpha* values in the .80 range; the discipline subscale has an *alpha* value of .77. Factor analyses generally support the seven subscales; however, the discipline subscale appears to incorporate two disciplinary components including both the presentation of behavioral guidance as well as presentation of consequences related to non-compliance. Taken as a whole, using factor analysis, approximately 47% of the variance is accommodated for by the seven subscale factors.

The PBIQ-R assessment tool is comprehensive, measuring both positive and negative parenting behaviors, as well as developmentally sensitive. An additional advantage of the PBIQ-R is that it can be completed by parents as well as, with modest instructional modifications, non-parents. This measure has substantial potential for intervention, especially parent behavior consultation and intervention with age appropriate levels from infancy through adulthood. Further, the measure may be utilized, with the theory, as a basis for the development of parent education programs, different types of assessments (e.g., clinical, forensic, pediatric), and monitoring the progress of individual and family therapy. For example, if a parent is experiencing difficulty with, or is under-appreciative of one or more of the parent roles (e.g., discipline, education), an intervention addressing development of the specific behaviors associated with that portion or those parts of the role can be developed.

Parent-Child Relationship Measures

Parent Child Relationship Inventory (PCRI)

In contrast to the parent behavior measures reviewed, the *Parent Child Relationship Inventory* (PCRI) was not developed to focus exclusively on parenting behaviors, but rather parent-child interactions and relationships. Gerard (1994) constructed the PCRI to measure mothers' and fathers' perceptions of their parent-child relationships from preschool age through adolescence. Five of the PCRI subscales are integral aspects of the parent-child relationship including satisfaction with parenting, parental involvement, communication, limit setting, and facilitation of child's autonomy (Coffman, Guerin, & Gottfied, 2006). The two additional subscales are related to parenting but not to the parent-child relationship; they measure parental support (i.e., amount of emotional support and practical assistance the parent receives) and role orientation (i.e., endorsement of shared or distinct roles for mothers and fathers). An advantage of the PCRI is that there are two validity scales (i.e., social desirability, inconsistency) which measure respondents' level of defensiveness and inconsistency.

There are 78 items which are rated on a scale from "1" strongly agree to "4" strongly disagree. Examples of items for the seven subscales include, "I worry a lot about money" for parental support, "I get as much satisfaction from having children as other parents do" for satisfaction with parenting, "I spend a great deal of time with my child" for involvement, "My child would say that I am a good listener" for communication, "I have trouble disciplining my child" for limit setting, "I can't stand the thought of my child growing up" for autonomy, and "Mothers who work are harming their children" for role orientation (Gerard, 1994).

Gerard (1994) does not rely on a theory of parenting interaction; instead, he developed the scale based on the analysis of potential items consistent with three basic parenting dimensions (i.e., affective, control, overcontrol/punishment). Gerard (1994) reports coefficient *alpha* levels are good, with no value below .70 and the median value at .82. More recently, Coffman et al. (2006) examined five of the seven subscales, finding that for their sample, coefficient *alpha* values of at least .70 were found for satisfaction with parenting, involvement, and limit setting, but not for communication or autonomy. Further, they caution PCRI use in custody evaluations since their research reveals differences in the correspondence between how adolescents view their relationship with their mothers as opposed to their fathers. That is, apparently there is more of a discrepancy in how fathers and adolescents perceive their dyadic relationship than between mothers and adolescents. As a result, they state that for custody evaluation, it is not appropriate to use a measure that is valid for one parent, but not for the other.

Parenting Relationship Questionnaire (PRQ)

Kamphaus and Reynolds (2006) focused on capturing parents' perspectives of the parent-child relationship in constructing their measure. Essentially, this instrument provides seven subscales which provide information regarding parenting style, parenting confidence, stress, and satisfaction with their child's school. The measure is utilized with parents of children 2 through 18 years of age (i.e., two levels: preschool, child/adolescent). The preschool scale has 45 items and the child/adolescent scale has 71 items; responses range from "0" never to "3" always. Examples of items include, "My child enjoys spending time with me" for attachment, "I listen to what my child has to say" for communication, "It is important for a child to follow family rules" for discipline, "My child and I play games together" for involvement, "I am in control of my household" for parenting confidence, "It's hard being a parent" for relational frustration, and "My child's school is run well" for satisfaction with school.

There is no specific parenting theoretical basis noted by the authors of this assessment measure (Kamphaus & Reynolds, 2006). Instead, this measure was designed to provide a concurrent measure of the parenting relationship to be tapped in conjunction with measures of the child's social-emotional functioning (e.g., BASC-2 measures). There is psychometric strength reported including internal consistency *alpha* estimates from .77 through .86 for the preschool measure and .78 to .93 for the child/adolescent scale. Test-retest reliabilities range from .72 to .89 and validity estimates, in terms of inter-correlations among the subscales, are moderate (Kamphaus & Reynolds, 2007). In addition, correlations with the PCRI are moderate and high PRQ relational frustration tends to be related to children's externalizing behaviors on the BASC-2. The manual lists numerous potential intervention options, including intervention/treatment programs, psycho-educational evaluations, clinical and pediatric evaluations, and family counseling and forensic evaluations.

Other Parenting Measures

Other parenting measures are found in the research literature that are also used in clinical practice. One such measure is the *Parenting Stress Index* (PSI; Abidin, 1983). This measure, like many other parenting measures, is not specifically based on a theory of parenting. Abidin developed this measure because of the association between parental stress and negative parenting behaviors. Factor analysis indicates that there are three sources of parental stress including those that reside in the parent (e.g., feeling incompetent or isolated), those that reside in the child (e.g., poor adaptability, high demandingness), and those residing in the parent-child relationship (e.g., unmet parental expectations).

Originally, this self-report measure consisted of 120 items, but it was shortened to 36 items so that it could be used as a screening instrument (*Parent Stress Index-Short Form*; PSI-SF). The PSI-SF also includes seven items that measure a parent's defensiveness. This measure has been used primarily with young children, specifically under age 10, thus limiting the clinical utility of this measure. Further, the PSI and PSI-SF were normed exclusively on mothers of children ages 1 to 12 years. This limits the usefulness of the scale as it cannot be generalized to fathers or children above 12 years of age. Since parents experience stress when their children are all ages, and this stress may lead to negative parenting behaviors, extending the norms upward would be beneficial (Abidin, 1983).

Recently, Chang and Fine (2007) report PSI-SF coefficient *alpha* levels of .79, .82, and .84 for the three subscales. Considering additional PSI-SF psychometric qualities, Haskett, Ahern, Ward, and Allaire (2006) examined factor structure and validity, finding support for a two factor model including Parent Distress (PD) and Child-Rearing Stress (CS) (e.g., includes items from the Parent-Child Dysfunctional Interaction and Difficult Child subscales). In addition, these researchers report evidence of PSI-SF construct and predictive validity as well as test-retest stability. In the end, Haskett et al. note that the CS scale, not the PD scale, predicts group status, since higher scores are associated with an increased chance of being in the abusive parent group.

Two additional measures were designed to specifically assess parenting in relation to Baumrind's parenting styles (i.e., permissive, authoritarian, and authoritative parenting) (Buri, 1991; Robinson, Mandleco, Olsen, & Hart, 1995). The first was developed by Buri and is called the *Parent Authority Questionnaire* (PAQ). This measure consists of 30 items with 10 items measuring each of the parenting styles. A unique aspect of this measure, when compared to others, is that it is completed by children. Specifically, older adolescents or young adults fill out one form based on how they recall their mother parented, and another on how they recall their father parented. The *Parent Authority Questionnaire-Revised* (PAQ-R) was later developed by Reitman, Rhode, Hupp, and Altobello (2002) for use as a parental self-report questionnaire where parents rated their own behavior. Test-retest and internal consistency were generally in the moderate range and there are some indications of discriminant-related and criterion-related validity.

Using three groups of participants, the PAQ-R was examined psychometrically and there is some doubt that the measure incorporates the three purported factors (i.e., authoritative, authoritarian, permissive) (Reitman et al., 2002). Indeed, the factor structure appears to vary according to sample characteristics (e.g., ethnicity, SES). The internal consistencies for the authoritarian and permissive subscales were modest and for the authoritative subscale weak. There are PAQ-R correlations with some PS subscales; for example, PAQ-R authoritativeness was associated with effective parent-child communication and authoritarian parenting was associated with overreactivity. With regard to the PCRI, however, authoritarian parenting was associated with communication and permissiveness was related to overreactivity. Clearly, additional research is needed to determine the PAQ-R psychometric characteristics and usefulness as a parenting research measure.

The second measure designed to measure Baumrind's parenting styles is the *Parenting Practices Questionnaire* (PPQ) developed by Robinson and colleagues (1995) for use with preschool age children. Again, this limits its utility. This measure also has two versions, both of which are completed by the parents. In one version, parents rate their own behavior, and in the other, they rate the behavior of their spouses. This format allows for increased reliability of obtained results as a parent's report of their own behavior can be compared to how their spouse rates their behavior. The PPQ consists of 62 items that relate to Baumrind's parenting styles. For example, one authoritative item is "I give praise when my child is good;" an authoritarian item is "I guide my child with punishment more than reason;" and a permissive item is "I state punishments to my child and do not actually do them." Factor analysis supported the structure of the three parenting styles, and delineated specific factors associated with each style. For example, authoritative parenting was associated with factors such as warmth and democratic participation, authoritarian parenting was associated with factors such as verbal hostility and directiveness, and permissive parenting was associated with factors such as lack of follow through and ignoring misbehavior (Robinson et al.; Lagace-Seguin & d'Entremont, 2006).

Recent research (Lagace-Seguin & d'Entremont, 2006), utilizing the PPQ indicates that authoritative parenting is negatively related to children's negative affect; whereas, both authoritarian and permissive parenting styles are positively related to children's negative affect.

Finally, based on extensive research showing that harsh and permissive parenting relates to children who are poorly behaved and aggressive; Arnold, O'Leary, Wolff and Acker (1993) developed the *Parenting Scale* (PS). This scale measures problematic parenting discipline styles that lead to externalizing problems in children. In terms of clinical practice, this measure is a cost-effective way of identifying parents with poor discipline strategies so that appropriate interventions can be used to improve disciplinary practices. The PS can also be used for research related to child behavior problems. The PS is a self-report scale that consists of 30 items and asks for the probability of the parents using different discipline strategies. Each item is based on parent discipline "mistakes" that theoretically relate to negative developmental outcomes (e.g., inconsistent punishment of inappropriate behavior) (Arnold et al.).

Originally, Arnold and his colleagues (1993) identified three dysfunctional discipline characteristics including laxness (i.e., permissive parenting), overreactivity (i.e., displays of anger, meanness, or irritability), and verbosity (i.e., lengthy verbal responses and a reliance on talking even when talking is ineffective). The overall scale demonstrated psychometric strength with high reliability coefficient *alphas* ranging from .63 for verbosity to .84 for the total scale. Later research found that the laxness and overreactivity factors held while the verbosity factor did not (Reitman et al., 2002). Rhoades and O'Leary (2007) confirmed the presence of the laxness and overreactivity factors with an additional hostile discipline factor (e.g., cursing, name-calling, physical punishment). They also found high *alpha* coefficients ranging from .78 to .85. In terms of validity, all three factors were related to children's behavior problems as reported on the CBCL (Achenbach, 1991).

Overall, parenting self-report measures have the potential to be cost-effective and provide practitioners with important information for diagnostic, case conceptualization, and intervention purposes. Each measure tends to have a somewhat different purpose, targets children of different ages in relation to parenting, utilizes different levels of theoretical and evidence-based support and psychometric strength, and possess different potential for intervention. The PBI, PBC, and PBIQ-R are all measures of parent behaviors, but they focus on different factors of parenting. The PBI focuses on support/engagement and hostility/coercion (Lovejoy et al., 1999). The PBC assesses a family's strengths and needs, and emphasizes expectations, discipline, and nurturing (Fox, 1994). The PBIQ-R captures a comprehensive picture of parenting because the measure taps bonding, discipline, education, general welfare and protection, responsivity, sensitivity, and negativity (Mowder, 2010; Mowder & Shamah, 2010).

The PCRI and PRQ are measures of parenting relationships. The PCRI focuses on parent-child interactions and relationships, while the PRQ provides information on parenting confidence, stress, and satisfaction with their child's school (Gerard, 1994; Kamphaus & Reynolds, 2006). Also, other measures reviewed in this article include the PSI, PAQ, PAQ-R, and PPQ. The PSI assesses parenting stress, and the PAQ, PAQ-R, and PPQ measure parenting styles such as permissive, authoritative, and authoritarian parenting (Abidin, 1983; Buri, 1991; Reitman et al., 2002; Robinson et al., 1995). As a result, there is no one parenting measure that addresses all parenting issues/concerns. Comprehensive knowledge on these measures is required for professional practice in school and clinic settings. More accurate and comprehensive assessments lead to more appropriate interventions for some children and families who need professional help. Assessing and determining specific parenting problems, however, is not enough for professionals to help individuals improve their parenting skills and styles. Parent interventions are equally important; effective and appropriate parent interventions have the potential to result in positive changes in some children's lives as well as improve family dynamics. Consequently, although this article is specifically focused on assessments, evidence-based interventions are presented briefly since parent assessment may lead to parent interventions.

Parent Interventions

Parent assessment sometimes leads to parent consultation and parent interventions. The issue of parent consultation is beyond the scope of this article, but a small sample of evidence-based parent interventions is offered as some indication of the range and scope of programs available. Since the issue of parent intervention or education is not the main focus of this article, readers are directed to the many references and internet sites associated with each of the three programs briefly reviewed.

Parent interventions differ in terms of the target of treatment (e.g., parent behavior, parenting relationship) and the use of theory and research. The issues of who is in the parenting role (e.g., biological parent, foster parent, grandparent), whether the services being offered represent prevention or intervention, the relevance of children's age and specific development needs (e.g., disabilities), individual versus group format, and multicultural sensitivity all form relevant concerns. In terms of evidence-based parent interventions, this article briefly reviews three: the Triple P-Parenting Program, The Incredible Years, and Adults and Children Together (ACT) Against Violence. These programs were selected on evidence-based support as well as applicability for parents of young children.

Triple P-Positive Parenting Program

The Triple P-Positive Parenting (Sanders, 1999; 2008) has as its central goal to develop individuals' capacity for self-regulation. Thus, the goals are to enhance parenting knowledge, skills, and confidence. The entire parenting program is based on behavioral theory, primarily social learning theory. The thrust of the program is to promote positive parenting in terms of establishing a safe environment and promoting a positive learning environment, helping the parent develop assertive discipline and realistic expectations, and sensitizing the parent to the importance and maintenance of self-care.

The Triple-P Positive Parenting Program includes five levels of intervention:

1. Level 1 involves all parents and utilizes media and health promotion campaign materials.

2. Level 2 includes parents wanting education or those parents who have specific concerns; this level involves parent support during routine well-child visits to health professionals.

3. Level 3 focuses on parents with concerns about their children who may need specific parent skill training; this level includes a brief program (80 minutes over four sessions) to manage a discrete problem behavior.

4. Level 4 targets parents who want intensive training regarding specific concerns about their children and parenting; this program involves 10 hours over 8-10 sessions targeting more behavioral concerns about children.

5. Level 5 includes parents with significant child/parenting concerns and these parents may be at-risk for maltreating their children; this program is intensive and individualized, with sessions of 60-90 minutes involving skills, mood management, and coping.

More specifically, examples of core parenting skills include giving descriptive praise, giving non-verbal attention, and providing engaging activities for children (Sanders, 2008). In terms of managing misbehavior, skills are taught involving establishing ground rules, using planned ignoring, and giving clear directions in a calm manner. Additional skills include spending quality time, talking with, and showing affection to children. In tandem with these skills are preparing parents to set a good example, using incidental teaching, and developing and utilizing behavior charts.

The evidence-base for Triple P-Parenting is impressive, representing approximately 30 years of development. A recent meta-analysis indicates that this program is effective (Nowak & Heinrichs, 2008). Outcomes were demonstrated through the assessment of different areas associated with the program, including parenting (e.g., PS), child problem behaviors (CBCL), relationships, and child anxiety and depression. The effect sizes for Levels 1 through 3 are generally smaller than for Levels 4 and 5 and, further, effect sizes are generally larger for mothers compared with fathers. The researchers had some difficulty determining whether the effect sizes were related more to the increase in positive behavior or the decrease in negative behavior. Regardless, the Triple P-Parenting exhibits a variety of strengths, such as a multi-level system of support generally based on behavior and social learning theory, significant effects reached at each of the 5 levels of intervention, flexibility in terms of multicultural dimensions of parenting, wide dissemination of the program, quality research, and associated public health implications.

The Incredible Years

The Incredible Years (Webster-Stratton, 2000) is another evidence-based parent education program. These materials present a series of parent education options which hold the goals of developing comprehensive treatment programs for young children with early-onset conduct problems as well as developing cost-effective, community-based, universal prevention programs that all families and teachers of young children can use to promote social competence and to prevent children from developing conduct problems. Thus, the general purpose is to prevent delinquency, drug abuse, and violence. In terms of reducing conduct problems in children, the program attempts to decrease negative behavior and noncompliance with parents at home and decrease peer aggression and disruptive behaviors in the classroom. Essentially, this program fosters social, emotional, and academic competence in children by seeking to increase children's social skills and understanding of feelings, increase children's conflict management skills, decrease negative attributions, and increase academic engagement, school readiness, and cooperation with teachers.

The Incredible Years provides five levels consistent with a pyramid approach (Webster-Stratton, 2000). The core of the program is called BASIC and involves 12 to 14 weeks of training. In terms of parent education, this curriculum assists parents in ways to play with their children, help children learn, monitor children's activities, and employ effective discipline techniques. The BASIC program can be added to the ADVANCE and SCHOOL parenting curricula. The curriculum provides additional training in areas such as anger management and communication. More specifically, the levels of training are as follows:

1. Level 1: The Baby Program includes 8 weekly sessions (6 weeks to 12 months of age), the Toddler Program includes 12 weekly sessions (1 – 3 year olds), and the School Readiness Program includes 4 weekly sessions (3 – 5 year olds).

2. Level 2: The BASIC Early Childhood Prevention Program involves 14 weekly sessions (3 – 6 years), the teacher classroom management program (TCM) includes 5 – 6 days monthly, and the classroom Dinosaur School (preschool, kindergarten, grades 1 and 2) involves 60 lessons with two per week.

3. Level 3: The Baby and Toddler Programs involve 20 weeks (0 – 3 year olds), the Level 2 BASIC Early Childhood Complete Program (3 - 6 years) involves 18-20 weekly parent guidance sessions and Universal TCM Training.

4. Level 4: The Level 2 BASIC Early Childhood or School-Age Programs include 16 - 18 sessions (6 -12 years), the Advanced Parent Program involves 8 - 12 parent guidance sessions, child pull-out therapy sessions in school (10 – 20 sessions), and teacher consultation.

5. Level 5: The BASIC Parenting, complete programs involve 16 - 18 sessions, Advanced Parent Program (8 - 12 sessions), and therapeutic child treatment in group sessions (20 2-hour sessions).

The Incredible Years has a wide array of written and other visual materials associated with the program. The materials offer a variety of parent education opportunities in terms of, for instance, praise and rewards as well as handling misbehavior and offering modeling opportunities for positive parenting behaviors.

Adults and Children Together (ACT) Against Violence

The Adults and Children Together (ACT) Against Violence training program was developed, based on psychological research, by the American Psychological Association (APA) in collaboration with the National Association for the Education of Young Children (NAEYC) (APA, 2002). The specific focus of the program is violence prevention toward young children by offering violence prevention materials to parents and early childhood professionals. Using a dissemination model, the program seeks to prepare professionals who, in turn, offer the violence prevention preparation to individuals and groups in the community. The program includes four units on anger management, social problem-solving, discipline, and media literacy.

The ACT program is theoretically based on social learning theory and the research-based curriculum is designed to help families and caregivers raise children without violence (APA, 2002). Basic information on child development is provided, along with what behaviors are consistent with different age levels. In addition, there are materials regarding risk factors for violence as well as the consequences of violence for young children's lives. The program itself is administered by certified ACT Facilitators in 2 – hour sessions for a minimum of 8 weeks. At the parenting classes, participants receive carefully prepared materials, including fact sheets, booklets, and a handbook in either English or Spanish.As an example, the ACT program provides alternatives for when a child misbehaves, suggesting that parents let children know what the expectations are with simple statements like, "Please put away your toys right now" (APA, 2002). Further, to give warnings and reminders, without threats, the suggestion is to say, "When you put away your toys, then you can go outside with your friends." With regard to discipline, the ACT program indicates that parents may ignore children's behavior which is irritating, take away a privilege once a child is old enough to understand the consequences of an action, let consequences teach lessons as long as the child's safety is not at risk, and utilize timeout as an opportunity for a short cooling off period or brief break.

Summary

In summary, parent assessment is an essential component of providing relevant services to young children and their families. Although there is no recognized standard for including parent assessments in evaluations for child-oriented services, there are a number of measurement instruments available. Parenting self-report measures are cost-effective and user friendly. However, they serve different purposes and are supported by various theories or parenting definitions. The measures also tend to have different degrees of psychometric and theoretical support, and result in somewhat dissimilar potential interventions. Practitioners need comprehensive knowledge about parenting measures in order to assure the use of measures consistent with the goals of assessment and other aspects of professional practice. Future directions for parenting assessment should focus on broadening and effectively adapting parenting measures to school and clinic settings. The instruments, in conjunction with other information regarding children and their families, have the potential to enhance professional understanding of needs and assist in tailoring interventions appropriately. Beyond assessment instruments, there are a number of excellent parent education programs, only three of which are presented briefly in this article. To be sure, future directions for intervention should aim at promoting and applying programs that are evidence-based. Coordinating assessment and intervention services to meet the needs of young children and their families is in the best interests of those families, their communities, and society as a whole.

References

Abidin, R. (1983). *The Parenting Stress Index*. Charlottesville, VA: Pediatric Psychology Press.

Achenbach, T. M. (1991). *Manual for the Child Behavior Checklist/4-19 and 1991 Profile*. Burlington: University of Vermont Department of Psychiatry.

American Psychological Association (2002). *ACT Training Program Workshop Manual*. Washington, D.C..: American Psychological Association.

Arnold, D. S., O'Leary, S. G., Wolf, L. S., & Acker, M. M. (1993). The Parenting scale: A measure of dysfunctional parenting in discipline situations. *Psychological Assessment, 5*, 137-144.

Bavolek, S. J. (1984). *Handbook for the Adult-Adolescent Parenting Inventory*. Eau Claire, WI: Family Development Resources.

Brook, J. S., Zheng, L., Whiteman, M., & Brook, D. W. (2001). Aggression in toddlers: Associations with parenting and marital relations. *Journal of Genetic Psychology, 162* (2), 228-241.

Buri, J. R. (1991). Parental Authority Questionnaire. *Journal of Personality Assessment, 57*(1), 110-119.

Chang, Y., & Fine, M. A. (2007). Modeling parenting stress trajectories among low-income young mothers across the child's second and third years: Factors accounting for stability and change. *Journal of Family Psychology, 21*(4), 584-594.

Coffman, J. K., Guerin, D. W., & Gottfried, A. W. (2006). Reliability and validity of the Parent Child Relationship Inventory (PCRI): Evidence from a longitudinal cross-informant investigation. *Psychological Assessment, 18*, 209-214.

Collins, W. A., Maccoby, E. E., Steinberg, L., Hetherington, E. M., & Bornstein, M. (2000). Contemporary research on parenting: The case for nature and nurture. *American Psychologist, 55*(2), 218-232.

Dallaire, D. H., Pineda, A. Q., Cole, D. A., Ciesla, J. A., Jacquez, F., LaGrange, B., et al. (2006). Relation of positive and negative parenting to children's depressive symptoms. *Journal of Clinical Child and Adolescent Psychology, 35*(2), 194-202.

Del Vecchio, T., & O'Leary, S. G. (2006). Antecedents of toddler aggression: Dysfunctional parenting in mother-toddler dyads. *Journal of Clinical Child and Adolescent Psychology, 35* (2), 194-202.

Fox, R. (1994). *Parent Behavior Checklist Manual*. Austin, TX: Pro-Ed.

Gerard, A. B. (1994). *Parent-Child Relationship Inventory (PCRI): Manual*. Los Angeles:Western Psychological Services.

Haskett, M. E., Ahern, L. S., Ward, C. S., & Allaire, J. C. (2006). Factor structure and validity of the Parenting Stress Index-Short Form. *Journal of Clinical Child and Adolescent Psychology, 35* (2), 302-312.

Kamphaus, R. W., & Reynolds, C. R. (2006). *Parenting Relationship Questionnaire.* Minneapolis, MN: Pearson.

Kamphaus, R. W., & Reynolds, C. R. (2007). *BASC-2 Behavioral and Emotional Screening System.* Retrieved from Mental Measurements Yearbook database.

Lagace-Seguin, D. G., & d'Entremont, M. L. (2006). The role of child negative affect in the relations between parenting styles and play. *Early Child Development and Care,* 176(5), 461-477.

Lovejoy, M., Weis, R., O'Hare, E., & Rubin, E. (1999). Development and initial validation of the Parent Behavior Inventory. *Psychological Assessment, 11*(4), 534-545.

Marcus, R. F., & Sanders-Reio, J. (2001). The influence of attachment on school completion. *School Psychology Quarterly, 16,* 427-444.

Mowder, B. A. (1994). Consultation with families of young at risk and handicapped children. *Journal of Educational and Psychological Consultation, 5,* 309 320.

Mowder, B. A. (2010). *Manual for Parent Behavior Importance Questionnaire-Revised (PBIQ-R) and Parent Behavior Frequency Questionnaire-Revised (PBFQ-R).* Under review.

Mowder, B. A., Harvey, V. S., Moy, L., & Pedro, M., (1995). Parent role characteristics: Parent views and their implications for school psychologists. *Psychology in the Schools, 32,* 27 37.

Mowder, B. A., Harvey, V. S., Pedro, M., Rossen, R., & Moy, L. (1993). Parent Role Questionnaire: Psychometric characteristics. *Psychology in the Schools, 30,* 248 254.

Mowder, B. A., & Shamah, R. (2010). Parent Behavior Importance Questionnaire-Revised (PBIQ-R): Scale development and psychometric characteristics. *Journal of Child and Family Studies.*

Nowak, C., & Heinrichs, N. (2008). A comprehensive meta-analysis of Triple P-Positive Parent Program using hierarchical linear modeling: Effectiveness and moderating variables. *Clinical Child and Family Psychology Review, 11,* 114-144.

Peters, C. L., & Fox, R. A. (1993). Parenting inventory: Validity and social desirability. *Psychological Reports, 72,* 683-689.

Reitman, D., Rhode, P. C., Hupp, S. D. A., & Altobello, C. (2002). Development and validation of the Parental Authority Questionnaire-Revised. *Journal of Psychopathology and Behavioral Assessment, 24,* 119-127.

Rhoades, K. A., & O'Leary, S. G. (2007). Factor Structure and Validity of the Parenting Scale. *Journal of Clinical Child and Adolescent Psychology, 36*(2), 137-146.

Robinson, C. C., Mandleco, B., Olsen, S. F., & Hart, C. H. (1995) Authoritative, authoritarian, and permissive parenting practices: Development of a new measure. *Psychological Reports, 77,* 819-830.

Ryan, R. M., Martin, A., & Brooks-Gunn, J. (2006). Is one good parent good enough? Patterns of mother and father parenting and child cognitive outcomes at 24 and 36 months. *Parenting: Science and Practice, 6,* 211-228.

Sanders, M. R. (1999). Triple P-Positive Parenting Program: Towards an empirically validated multilevel parenting and family support strategy for the prevention of behavior and emotional problems in children. *Clinical Child and Family Psychology Review, 2,* 71-90.

Sanders, M. R. (2008). Triple P-Positive Parenting Program as a public health approach to strengthening parenting. *Journal of Family Psychology, 22,* 506-517.

Webster-Stratton, C. (2000). *Incredible years: The parents, teachers, and children training series.* Seattle, WA: Carolyn Webster-Stratton.

Challenges and Considerations when Transitioning Preschoolers with Complex Medical Histories to Kindergarten

Marie E. Briody & Jacqueline M. Martone
Rusk Institute of Rehabilitation Medicine, NYU Langone Medical Center

The process of transitioning children with complex medical histories and special needs to classroom placements within the public education system is not a new phenomenon; the integration of these students into the mainstream schooling system began in the late 1970s. However, philosophies and teaching surrounding the education of children with special needs have continued to evolve and shift over the years and the concept of integration remains controversial. While school resources, therapeutic services in the schools, and special education initiatives have improved over the last several decades to meet the needs of these children, the process of finding the most appropriate placement continues to be a challenge for both transition teams and families. This article explores the history of special education integration, the transition process and common challenges that arise throughout the process. Lastly, two cases will be presented that highlight the process for two children with very different profiles.

Keywords: Pre-school, disabilities, children with special needs, transition, kindergarten

Children with complex medical histories and special needs, for which there is a myriad of potential etiologies (e.g., cerebral palsy, brain injury, genetic disorders, and cancer), encounter significant challenges when transitioning through the education system (Janus, Lefort, Cameron, & Kopechankski, 2007). The needs of these children often overlap with children in mainstream education, including providing opportunities for social and academic growth; however, these children also present with additional considerations, such as medical, therapeutic, and unique developmental needs that should be considered when exploring academic placements. While the process of transitioning children with special needs to a classroom placement within the public education system is not a new phenomenon, as the integration of these students into the mainstream schooling

All correspondence should be addressed to: Marie E. Briody, Ph.D., Rusk Institute of Rehabilitation Medicine, 400 East 34th Street, Suite RR-509, New York, New York 10016. Electronic mail may be sent to: Marie.Briody@nyumc.org.

system began in the late 1970s, there continues to be gaps in the system. Even though the process of transitioning these students has been conducted for nearly 40 years, there remains a paucity of research and guidance in this arena to help address the common challenges encountered by parents and transition teams (i.e., groups of professionals which may include a psychologist, social worker, therapists from related services, teachers, and school administration members who assist in transitioning a student from one setting to another).

The Education for All Handicap Children Act (1975) required that all children be educated in the least restrictive environment, suggesting that children that were once readily placed in self-contained classrooms should spend as much time as possible in mainstream classrooms with adaptations and appropriate special education supports (Madden & Slavin, 1983). While the model for integration has many benefits and positive outcomes related to both social and academic development (Calhoun & Elliott, 1977; Cassidy & Stanton, 1959; Hanline & Murray, 1984), there are also many challenges encountered and considerations for the team to appreciate when working through the transition process. In fact, experienced educators have found the task of transitioning special needs children to other settings to be an overwhelming and demanding one (Jewett et al., 1998). While there is some research reflecting on the process from the perspectives of both families and teachers (Fowler, Schwartz, & Atwater, 1991; Jewett et al., 1998), there remains a limited amount of information on challenges faced and issues to consider as a transition team.

The Benefits of Integration

There have been a few historically significant studies looking at the social and academic outcomes of the integration model specifically in regard to educating children who are medically complex and have special needs together with general education students (Calhoun & Elliott, 1977; Cassidy & Stanton, 1959; Leinhardt, 1980; Madden & Slavin, 1983). Much of the early work focused on the academic outcomes of mainstreaming students with special needs and the results demonstrated new perspectives on the subject. Specifically, the studies that compared children in various special education classrooms (e.g., contained classrooms, integrated classroom) showed significant differences in the students' achievement over time depending on the classroom placement (Calhoun & Elliott; Cassidy & Stanton). There were several benefits to the integration model which encompassed a more holistic view of the child's developmental progress. The pioneering review that initiated efforts to evaluate such integrated outcomes was lead by Madden and Slavin. Specifically, their early research found that, from a social-emotional perspective, students with special needs who were integrated in a general education classroom, with the appropriate supports, demonstrated higher self-esteem and more appropriate behavior. From a cognitive perspective, students with more mild learning difficulties performed significantly better in terms of IQ when placed in mainstream classrooms when compared with peers in self-contained classrooms. Although this effect on cognitive potential was not found in students with more severe handicaps, the findings regarding social-emotional functioning provide powerful implications. Even when a full-day integration model is not appropriate, a partial day integration model may work well, particularly for its social value. Hanline and Murray (1984) discuss the specific benefits related to integrating a child with special needs into a portion of a typical child's school day, such as during lunchtime or through peer tutoring, and how these encounters may serve as a valuable experience for both students with and without special needs.

A more recent study which reviewed inclusion programs in eight schools found generally positive outcomes in regard to both the general education students and students with special needs (Idol, 2006). Specific areas assessed in the study included teacher and student attitudes toward students with disabilities, as well as general education students' academic and social performance. Positive teacher attitudes, adequate teacher support from an administrative level, and in-class resource personnel were cited as key factors in effective inclusion programs (Idol, 2006; Leatherman & Niemeyer, 2005; Weiner, 2003).

Difficulties with the Current Transition System

While the idea and practice of integrating students with special needs can be a successful model, there are several logistical difficulties encountered, such as determining appropriate placement and advocating for the appropriate services and supports (Fowler et al., 1991; Janus et al., 2007). While the process is centrally governed within school districts and led by a special education committee that provides evaluations, appropriate service determinations and placement recommendations, there are invariably kinks and hurdles throughout the process that transition teams often encounter (Fowler et al.; Janus et al.).

The transition from preschool to kindergarten can be challenging and stressful for families with typically developing children, as this period of time represents a child's growing independence (Fowler et al., 1991). However, there are additional challenges associated with transitioning a child with special needs that require ample time for planning, support from a transition team, and thoughtful consideration and anticipation of a child's often complex needs and capabilities to ensure their eventual placement in an adequately challenging, yet supportive setting. The following is an exploration of the commonly faced challenges experienced by the transition team at a therapeutic-based preschool program, as well as important factors to be considered throughout the transition process to kindergarten.

Challenges and Considerations for Transitioning

Overview of the Transition Process

The process of transitioning preschool students with special needs to kindergarten is a complex, multi-faceted, and collaborative team effort in working with parents and families to find a program that best meets their child's medical, therapeutic, developmental, social, and learning needs (Fowler et al., 1991; Janus et al., 2007).

Although a transition system has not been implemented on a nationwide scale, a strategic transition process was developed by Project TEEM (Transition into Elementary Education Mainstream) at the University of Vermont and assists public school systems in establishing transition teams for preschool students entering elementary education (Conn-Powers, Ross-Allen & Holburn, 1990; Fowler et al., 1991). This "system" sets forth a series of guidelines to assist with smooth transitions and primarily includes the following points: (a) individualized and collaborative planning between parents and school staff, (b) family support, and (c) preparation for transition with the student and follow-up after the transition (Conn-Powers et al.; Fowler et al.). While this model encompasses the main points to focus on during the transition period, there are often still challenges in determining who plays each role on the transition team, in addition to variability in schedules and methods for implementing the above stated model. Additionally, while the above process is ideal it may not be evidenced in everyday practice as not all districts require this and the requirements vary city to city and state to state.

While there are variations in requirements, all states include processes for the provision of special education services. The need for special education services is generally assessed through evaluations, school observation and assessment of academic records and teacher reports in order to help determine an appropriate placement and services, which are then formalized and documented through an Individualized Education Program (IEP).

The nature of the transition process can be quite difficult and trying for families and children; therefore, medical centers with therapeutic-based preschool classrooms (i.e., preschools that provide therapeutic services on-site) often create their own transition teams as a means of facilitating the process and meeting the families' needs on a more individual basis. One example of a medical center transition team includes members from educational, therapeutic, and medical disciplines, such as psychologists, social workers, physical therapists, occupational therapists, speech therapists, teachers, and school administrators. Each individual discipline conducts an evaluation and provides a written report of the child's continued needs, documenting goals and requesting continued services be a part of the child's updated IEP. Additionally, each child is evaluated by the psychologist on the team who conducts an assessment of the child's cognitive abilities, pre-academic and adaptive skills.

After evaluations have been conducted, clinical staff on the team partner with families in sharing information about the child's functioning as well as assessing the family's goals and expectations for their child. The team then meets together as a comprehensive group to discuss the child's continued needs, areas for growth, and potential barriers to success in hopes of helping to recommend an appropriate placement. Parents are informed as to the process of identifying and visiting schools which may be appropriate in meeting their child's individual needs. While staff members often provide liaison services to families in order to help them navigate the educational system, a crucial component of the process is empowering parents to be strong advocates for their child by informing them and involving them in the necessary processes and procedures.

While families are provided with the support and knowledge from the transition team in order to navigate the special education process, many parents embark on this process on an individual basis and do not have adequate support. Inadequate parent support due to a lack of advocacy skills is cited as a barrier to effective transitions (Janus et al., 2007). Other barriers cited include inadequate time and funds on the part of the sending program in order to coordinate the transition most effectively (Fowler et al., 1991).

Considerations for Acquired vs. Congenital Disabilities

While all families that have children with special needs or complex medical histories face similar challenges when transitioning through the educational system, there are some differences that may affect needs and future care based on whether the medical condition is acquired (e.g., traumatic or delayed onset) versus congenital (e.g., diagnosed prenatally or at birth). More specifically, family coping strategies, levels of family and parent stress, and the nature of the child's condition (e.g., degenerative versus acute) can each impact decisions regarding placement (Kazak & Marvin, 1984; Ray, 2003). For children with congenital or degenerative conditions, parents may have had more time to plan and prepare for their child's needs and acclimate themselves with the available services and supports their child requires. Parents of children with congenital or degenerative conditions may be focused on providing them with an ongoing supportive and therapeutic setting that can best meet their child's needs and challenges as they continue to evolve. However, parents of a child with a condition of a traumatic or acute nature may have different concerns regarding their child's education as their needs may be temporary. Families who have children with acquired or traumatic conditions also have the challenge of being in a position where they suddenly have to learn about the new challenges and needs of their child, as well as incorporate these needs and challenges into their family system and community life. Thus, parents may need different levels of support throughout the process, such as parent support groups, educational advocacy or individual counseling to promote coping and family resilience (Miller, Gordon, Daniele, & Diller, 1992; Smith, Oliver, & Innocenti, 2001).

When working with a family throughout the transition process, it is important not only to consider the nature of the child's disability and his or her individual developmental, medical and learning needs, but other factors as well. Specifically, the unique stressors and coping styles of the family, family constellation and impact on siblings and other family members, cultural considerations, and caregiver goals and values should be considered when working with children and families (Zaccario, Salsberg, Gordon, & Bilginer, 2009). All of these factors along with knowledge of the local education system and associated resources for children with special needs are crucial in assessing an appropriate placement.

Issues Related to Determining a Child's Cognitive Ability

Determining the cognitive ability of a typically developing young child is often a difficult task given the varied rate of general development (Missiuna & Samuels, 1989). However, this issue becomes even more challenging when working with children who have complex medical histories and special needs. These children may present with uneven skill development across cognitive and developmental domains and also may have impairments in the sensory and communicative modalities often used to assess abilities in young children (Baumeister, 1984; Missiuna & Samuels, 1989). The use of standardized measures of assessment is significantly limited in assessing this population as well as those who are not primarily English language speakers. Thus, the psychologist's clinical judgment and qualitative observations play a very important role in both the assessment and interpretation, so as to capture the child's true abilities and potential without minimizing their needs and areas of vulnerability.

Traditional measures of cognitive ability for preschool-aged children, such as the *Wechsler Preschool and Primary Scale of Intelligence – Third Edition* (WPPSI-III) and the *Stanford-Binet Intelligence Scales – Fifth Edition* (SB5), typically involve a language component on both the verbal and non-verbal measures. For example, to determine an intelligence quotient (IQ), children are required to respond verbally on measures within the verbal domain and even on some tasks within the non-verbal domain, children must be able to comprehend oral instructions in order to understand the task demand (Roid, 2003; Wechsler, 2002). As such, a child who is primarily non-verbal or who has language processing difficulties may not be able to demonstrate their capabilities on these types of assessments with language requirements. Thus, the clinician in this scenario must rely upon alternative measures of non-verbal intelligence that do not require verbal output in addition to very limited amounts of language-based instructions, such as the *Primary Test of Non-verbal Intelligence* (PTONI). This type of assessment measures a young child's reasoning abilities and is useful for testing children who are non-verbal or who present with motor challenges (Ehrler & McGhee, 2008). Given the challenges that can present when assessing children who are medically complex, it remains the clinician's responsibility to utilize an instrument that can best capture the child's abilities to ensure that their academic placement provides the most academically challenging, yet least restrictive environment that is suited to meet their needs and match their cognitive potential. An example of such difficulties in assessment is discussed in the second case study.

The Impact of the Variability in Child's Skills and Abilities

As discussed above, there are several factors that can impact a child's ability to demonstrate their cognitive and academic abilities with standard assessment measures. These factors can include physical limitations and impairments, speech and language impairments, visual impairments, and hearing impairments. Not only can these limitations impact a child's ability to demonstrate the skills that they do have, but they can also impact the ways they learn in the classroom setting. Thus, it is the treating therapist's and transition team's role to determine the extent of the child's limitations that may preclude them from certain placements and their strengths that can help them succeed across different settings.

For example, children with significant physical limitations, such as in spastic quadraparesis cerebral palsy or spina bifida with mild cognitive impairments, may require additional support surrounding their physical needs in the school setting, such as specialized seating and positioning equipment and augmentative communication devices that allow them to participate more fully in classroom activities. However, they may also demonstrate the cognitive abilities and learning potentials that warrant a more challenging academic curriculum, and placement with appropriate social peers is always a consideration. Thus the transition team must determine the child's needs as a whole and work to find an appropriate setting that incorporates the child's needs and limitations from a holistic approach, and often such placements are not easily found.

Issues to Consider When Preparing Students for Transition

A common issue that may arise when transitioning children with complex medical needs is balancing academic preparation for kindergarten with therapeutic needs. While children in therapeutic pre-school settings require intensive therapy throughout the school day, they often miss a significant amount of the "school day." As a result, children in these settings often have delayed or uneven mastery of pre-academic skills and concepts for several reasons including: gaps in their education secondary to medical complications, time devoted to therapies, and being placed in a setting which needs to accommodate children of various cognitive levels. Therefore, an important part of the preparation process includes practice with pre-academic skills, which can be achieved through academic skills groups that include children preparing to advance to a community setting or kindergarten placement.

While studies have examined the readiness skills required to promote success in kindergarten for typically developing preschoolers (Graziano et al., 2007; Logue, 2007), Carta and colleagues conducted a study to evaluate "essential classroom survival skills" specifically in preschool students with disabilities that would later determine success in kindergarten (Carta, Atwater, Schwartz, & Miller, 1990). The study identified three primary skills: (a) successful completion of "within the classroom" transitions (e.g., the ability to independently transition between activities), (b) participation in large instructional groups, and (c) the ability to complete a task or assignment independently. Most importantly, follow-up data from this study revealed that children who received the interventions to hone these "essential" skills were more likely to go on to mainstreamed kindergarten versus controls. Thus, the identified school survival skills that promote positive classroom participation and individual work ethic are important to address and facilitate in preschoolers with special needs who are preparing for kindergarten (Fowler et al., 1991).

Other important issues that may surface within the social domain are awareness of disability, social competence, and differences between people (Rosenkoetter, Hains, & Fowler, 1994). For the most part, many children in a therapeutic preschool program are functioning within a protected environment where each child has a different type or level of disability. However, for children transitioning to a community preschool setting or integrated preschool classroom, this may be their first experience interacting with typically developing peers. Several social competence skills have been identified as directly related positive outcomes in school success including self-help skills, interpersonal skills, and social communication skills (Kemp & Carter, 2005).

Parents also have complex feelings and concerns around this topic, particularly in regard to issues of peer acceptance (Janus et al., 2007). Therefore an important part of the transition curriculum should include issues related to individual differences, respect, comfort level in sharing about one's individual differences and respecting differences in others, as these children may encounter socially-related challenges upon integration.

Lastly, in exploring which type of placement may be best for a child, the family's priorities, resources, and any potential barriers to collaborate with the school should be considered. For example, if determining whether a local public school placement is best for a child, as opposed to a private or specialized placement, clinicians must consider not only how accessible the private placement may be (e.g., how long will the child be traveling to school), but also the potential effect on the child's extracurricular social development as play-dates may be harder to arrange when children are not living where they attend school. Additionally, caregivers may have a harder time collaborating with school staff and attending school functions if the school is located far from their residence. In regard to accessing related services, for some families, it may be more important to have in-school access to therapies rather than place more emphasis on the specific classroom constellation or curriculum as some caregivers are not able to bring their child to therapies after school. In other scenarios, it may be most important to caregivers to have all of their children attending the same school. This is not to say that the goal of identifying a medically and academically appropriate placement should not be strived for, but the family's needs, values and preferences also must be considered in exploring placement options.

Case Illustrations

The following two case examples illustrate some of the common challenges encountered throughout the transition process. The first case involves a young girl with a medically complex history who has been diagnosed with cancer with both physical and cognitive sequelae secondary to her chemotherapy treatment regimen. The second case involves another young girl who was diagnosed with cerebral palsy at birth and presents with significant variability between her physical and cognitive abilities. Both children are students in a self-contained, medically-based, therapeutic preschool.

Case Example 1: A Complex Medical History

This first case involves a 5-year-old Haitian-American female, with a complex medical history. She will be referred to as "Abby." Abby was initially diagnosed with a left temporal juvenile pilocytic astrocytoma (JPA)[1] at 2 ½ years of age, which was subsequently resected and treated with a high-dose chemotherapy regimen. Abby initially presented with unsteady gait and right hemiparesis in both her upper and lower extremities. Her classroom consisted of a 9:1:2 student-teacher-assistant ratio and she received speech and language, psychological, occupational, and physical therapies in the school setting through both "push-in" (e.g., therapist joins classroom) and "pull-out" (e.g., child leaves classroom) sessions. Given her continued chemotherapy treatment regimens, Abby attended school 4 days per week and received her treatments on the fifth day of the week outside of school. Abby wore a soft, protective helmet for safety when walking both inside and outside of the classroom, as well as a right ankle foot orthotic (AFO) for stability.

Abby's social-emotional functioning was generally appropriate within the classroom setting, with some tendencies towards socially immature and attention-seeking behaviors. Abby also demonstrated difficulties with transitions between therapies, as well as at the beginning and end of the school day. In the classroom, Abby enjoyed participating in classroom activities and

---

[1] A benign neoplasm (tumor) that can produce varying effects depending on its location in the brain. More specifically, the surgical resection of Abby's left temporal tumor resulted in right-sided hemiparesis (weakness), as the left side of the brain controls the right side of the body.

acting as her teacher's helper, although at times she was easily distracted by self-directed interests. Additionally, Abby demonstrated difficulties attending to tasks that required individual effort, as she tends to move off task easily without one-on-one support (a potential side effect of her treatment). In counseling, Abby demonstrated well-developed play skills, evidencing both imaginative (e.g., doctor, family, teacher) and reciprocal play, although she had difficulty following directions, respecting boundaries and transitioning back to the classroom.

Abby's cognitive profile revealed high average non-verbal reasoning skills and solidly average language and communication skills, demonstrating strong intellectual abilities and good potential for learning in a general education classroom. However, Abby's pre-academic skills were assessed to be delayed for age, as she had not yet grasped number and letter concepts, and had only a basic knowledge of shapes and colors. This discrepancy between her cognitive potential and her pre-academic skills may in part have been secondary to gaps in her preschool education due to medical treatments, the amount of time dedicated to various related therapies versus teaching of preacademic skills during the school day, her variable attention, and learning difficulties related to her treatment. Other notable areas of difficulty include Abby's fine and gross motor skills.

Overall, Abby was an intelligent, engaging, and resilient young girl who demonstrated strong cognitive potential, despite her complex medical history. In preparation for Abby's transition to kindergarten the following issues were considered by all members of her education and treatment team: (a) supporting her current medical and physical challenges as well as preparing for accommodations needed for potential future treatment, (b) protecting against risks for decreased self-confidence and self-esteem, (c) remediation of delayed pre-academic skills, (d) providing a challenging academic environment to match her cognitive potential, (e) providing a small and supportive environment to help with her attention-related skills, and (f) providing a social setting within the classroom with peers that could model age appropriate social skills.

In establishing Abby's IEP, her entire treatment team (i.e., psychologist, teacher, social worker, school principal, physical therapist, occupational therapist, speech and language therapist, and mother) met to discuss her progress thus far and considerations for her IEP moving forward. In addition, all of the concerns stated above were addressed and included in the discussion when determining an appropriate kindergarten placement. The team determined that Abby would continue to require all of her related services, to be provided in the school setting. It was also recommended that Abby continue to have access to psychological services throughout the transition process and her medical treatment, as integrating into a different educational setting is likely to raise some new issues related to her pre-morbid issues. A collaborative team teaching (CTT) classroom (e.g., integrated co-teaching) placement with related services was suggested for several reasons:

1. It was important to support Abby's strong cognitive potential and to be participating in an academically challenging environment.

2. The additional presence of a special education teacher in the classroom would provide the learning support and individualized attention that she may need in order to be successful in the school setting.

3. An integrated classroom would provide Abby with typically developing peers as well as peers with special needs.

4. It was important to place Abby in the least restrictive environment to promote her overall development.

In summary, this transition case highlights several factors and considerations when transitioning medically complex preschool students to kindergarten: their academic needs, cognitive skills, the least restrictive setting they can succeed in, social needs, therapeutic needs, and social-emotional needs.

Case Example 2: A Variable Profile

"Kate" is a 4-year, 5-month-old girl who has spastic quadriplegic cerebral palsy. She currently attends a therapeutic preschool program, and per her IEP, she is placed in a 9:1:2 classroom and receives speech and language therapy for 30 minutes three times weekly, physical therapy for 30 minutes three times weekly, and occupational therapy for 30 minutes four times weekly within her preschool setting.

Briefly, Kate's developmental and medical history is significant for prematurity (28 week gestation) and an extended neonatal intensive care unit (NICU) stay. Developmental milestones were delayed. Kate is a sweet and good-natured girl who presents with significant physical and speech challenges. Kate is unable to sit or walk independently, although she can sit with support, and requires assistance for feeding. She is able to reach for a switch and consistently use a yes/no switch board to communicate her needs. Although Kate is verbal, she is only able to produce generally one or two words at a time and she is significantly dysarthric, making her speech difficult to understand.

In spite of her challenges in other areas of development, Kate's social-emotional functioning is generally age appropriate within the classroom setting. Kate enjoys participating in activities and being an active member of the class. She gets along well with her classmates and enjoys welcoming therapists and visitors into the classroom with a friendly "hi" and big smile. While Kate does have difficulty with articulation and may not always speak up in a busy classroom, she is in fact absorbing an abundance of information that she is eager to share.

In assessing Kate's abilities, it was challenging to choose an assessment that would capture her abilities given her language and motor difficulties. Standardized intelligence tests for this age group rely both on motor manipulation as well as language abilities, both areas of vulnerability for Kate. Additionally, utilizing a standard developmental assessment tool would only highlight her areas of challenge. As such, specific subtests from a standard IQ measure were administered as well as subtests from a measure designed to assess concepts and pre-academic skills associated with school readiness. In addition to Kate's motor and speech difficulties, Kate also presented with variable attention and perceived motivation, possibly due to the effortful process required of her in order to respond to test items. However, she is so socially motivated that Kate was easily encouraged to persevere with testing with praise and social reinforcement.

Despite her challenges, Kate performed within the low average to average range across the tasks administered. While characterized by difficulties with articulation, Kate was able to name several pictures of common objects and demonstrate her knowledge of information as well as various pre-academic concepts. Many of the tasks presented required only a single word response, which facilitated Kate's performance; however, it is likely that she possesses more knowledge than she is able to communicate at this time.

In sum, Kate was an engaging, playful, and capable young girl who demonstrated good cognitive abilities and future learning potential. Secondary to her cerebral palsy, Kate had significant articulation or oral-motor difficulties. While Kate had a good single-word vocabulary, her speech was often difficult to understand for the untrained ear. Areas of consideration in planning for her kindergarten placement included identifying a placement that will accommodate her medical and therapy needs as well providing adequate academic and social stimulation. The biggest challenge for those working with Kate was determining her understanding of concepts and facilitating her communication. Kate was a social and engaging child who loves to share and her current limitations in communication impact her learning, socialization, sense of efficacy and overall well-being. As such, ongoing efforts at developing her mastery with alternative/ assistive communication devices were crucial.

As far as specific placement recommendations, the team felt that Kate should be placed in a small, structured, and supportive kindergarten setting that would foster her learning and communication as well as be able to meet her significant and ongoing therapeutic needs. A small program was recommended to optimize Kate's attention and availability for more individualized attention throughout the day, and a structured program, such as the one she currently attends, seems to help Kate internalize and predict classroom routines and expectations, thus promoting increased participation. Additionally, specific physical considerations in such a setting might include wheelchair accessibility, ample room to accommodate positioning and seating equipment, the availability of therapeutic support via occupational, physical, and speech therapy services onsite, which would allow for therapists to treat Kate within her school setting with peers as well as provide "push-in" services.

There is such a specialized program available in the geographic area in which she lives that provides an integrated academic environment designed specifically for students who have significant limitations in mobility but who possess generally average cognitive and learning capacity. As an integrated or inclusion program, this placement includes children without special needs and was recommended as an ideal option for Kate, particularly given her strong social interest and cognitive ability. However, enrollment in this program is limited. Alternatively, given her high level of need for ongoing access to specialized equipment and therapeutic interventions, continuing in a self-contained program for her kindergarten placement was suggested. Specialized consideration should be given to her communication needs and efforts at identifying effective augmentative communication devices and interventions should be available.

Case Examples Summary

While each case illustration depicts the story of a child who has special considerations in transitioning to kindergarten, Abby and Kate possess very different developmental profiles with variable strengths, vulnerabilities, abilities, and challenges. While a good deal of thoughtful planning is put forth in making informed recommendations for kindergarten placement, in every case, it is important to note that an assessment of any young child offers only a snapshot of a moving picture. This is particularly true of children with medical complexities. As such, their academic, emotional and developmental needs require careful and frequent monitoring and assessment in order to provide ongoing and appropriate recommendations.

While the children from the case illustrations above have not yet transitioned to kindergarten, historically, our best outcomes have occurred when there has been early and careful coordination of efforts among the transition team, parents, and school system. In two recent successful transition cases, all parties were in agreement regarding the classroom recommendation and such a placement was available in the child's community school setting. Another factor that facilitated a positive outcome included ongoing communication between the parent and school system in preparation for the child's entry to the new school system. Parents and the transition team began exploring educational placements early and parents were active in reaching out and visiting potential schools. In one case, the mother set up a special visit to the new school to share a video about her child's difficulties and abilities to the staff and students so that they would be informed about the new student. This process facilitated both the child's and the school staff's comfort level about the student and provided an opportunity to share any concerns and learn about the new student's needs.

Discussion

In conclusion, while we continue to attempt to understand the complex needs of young children with medical considerations as a population, assessing and meeting the needs of these children with an appreciation for the diversity within this population and the uniqueness presented by each child continues to present challenges. This may be especially true depending upon the resources and academic provisions available in the child's community. In many cases, creativity and a team approach are especially crucial to ensure an appropriate placement. In every case, factors such as caregiver participation, staff support, a team approach, current assessments and an accurate understanding of the child's unique strengths and vulnerabilities, as well as an understanding of the transition process are all necessary factors to promote an optimal placement.

Additionally, future research efforts should aim at measuring outcomes for children with complex medical histories who are transitioned to various academic placements from self-contained or therapeutic academic settings. These outcomes should assess a variety of factors such as: (a) nature of child's medical concern, (b) parent involvement, (c) sending school's involvement, (d) type of academic setting transitioned from and to, as well as (e) psychosocial concerns such as socioeconomic status, cultural considerations/language, family size and coping resources and supports. As the literature suggests, and based on experience, the best outcomes are likely to occur when incorporating all of the aforementioned factors in deciding about a transition placement, along with a team approach and strong parent advocacy.

References

Baumeister, A. (1984). Some methodological and conceptual issues in the study of cognitive processes with retarded people. In P. H. Brooks, R. Sperber, & C. McCauley (Eds.), *Learning and Cognition in the Mentally Retarded* (pp. 1-38). Hillsdale, NJ: Erlbaum.

Calhoun, G., & Elliott, R. (1977). Self-concept and academic achievement of educable retarded and emotionally disturbed pupils. *Exceptional Children, 44,* 379-380.

Carta, J., Atwater, J., Schwartz, I., & Miller, P. (1990). Applications of ecobehavioral analysis to the study of transitions across early education settings. *Education and Treatment of Children, 13,* 298-315.

Cassidy, V., & Stanton, J. (1959). *An investigation of the factors involved in the educational placement of mentally retarded children.* Columbus, Ohio: Ohio State University Press.

Conn-Powers, M., Ross-Allen, J., & Holburn, S. (1990). Transition of young children into the elementary education mainstream. *Topics in Early Childhood Special Education, 9,* 91-105.

Ehrler, D. J., & McGhee, R. L. (2008). *Primary Test of Nonverbal Intelligence, Examiner's Manual.* Austin, TX: PRO-ED.

Fowler, S. A., Schwartz, I., & Atwater, J. (1991). Perspectives on the transition from preschool to kindergarten for children with disabilities and their families. *Exceptional Children, 58,* 136-145.

Graziano, P. A., Reavis, R. D., Keane, S. P., & Calkins, S. D. (2007). The role of emotion in children's early academic success. *Journal of School Psychology, 45,* 3-19.

Hanline, M. F., & Murray, C. (1984). Integrating severely handicapped children into regular public schools. *The Phi Delta Kappan, 66,* 273-276.

Idol, L. (2006). Toward inclusion of special education students in general education: A program evaluation of eight schools. *Remedial and Special Education, 27*(2), 77-94.

Janus, M., Lefort, J., Cameron, R., & Kopechankski, L. (2007). Transition issues for children with special needs. *Canadian Society for the Study of Education, 30,* 628–648.

Jewett, J., Tertell, L., King-Taylor, M., Parker, D., Tertell, L., & Orr, M. (1998). Four early childhood teachers reflect on helping children with special needs make the transition to kindergarten. *The Elementary School Journal, 98,* 329-338.

Kazak, A., & Marvin, R. (1984). Differences, difficulties, and adaptation: Stress and social networks in families with a handicapped child. Family Relations: *Journal of Applied Family & Child Studies, 33,* 67-77.

Kemp, C., & Carter, M. (2005). Identifying skills for promoting successful inclusion in kindergarten. *Journal of Intellectual & Developmental Disability, 30*(1), 31-44.

Leatherman, J. M. & Niemeyer, J. A. (2005). Teachers' attitudes toward inclusion: Factors influencing classroom practice. *Journal of Early Childhood Teacher Education, 26*, 23-36.

Leinhardt, G. (1980). Transition rooms: Promoting maturation or reducing education? *Journal of Educational Psychology, 72*, 55-61.

Logue, M. E. (2007). Early childhood learning standards: Tools for promoting social and academic success in kindergarten. *Children & Schools, 29*(1), 35-43.

Madden, N., & Slavin, R. (1983). Mainstreaming students with mild handicaps: Academic and social outcomes. *Review of Educational Research, 53*, 519-569.

Missiuna, C., & Samuels, M. (1989). Dynamic assessment of preschool children with special needs: Comparison of mediation and instruction. *Remedial and Special Education, 10*, 53-60.

Miller, C. A., Gordon, R. M., Daniele, R., & Diller, L. (1992). Stress, appraisal and coping in mothers of disabled and nondisabled children. *Journal of Pediatric Psychology, 17*, 587-605.

Morison, J. E., Bromfield, L. M., & Cameron, H. J. (2003). A therapeutic model for supporting families of children with a chronic illness or disability. *Child and Adolescent Mental Health, 8*, 125-130.

Ray, L. D. (2003). The social and political conditions that shape special-needs parenting. *Journal of Family Nursing, 9*, 281-304.

Roid, G. H. (2003b). *Stanford-Binet Intelligence Scales: Fifth Edition, Examiner's Manual*. Itasca, IL: Riverside.

Rosenkoetter, S., Haines, A., & Fowler, S. A. (1994). *Bridging early services for children with special needs and their families*. Baltimore: Paul H. Brookes.

Smith, T., Oliver, M., & Innocenti, M. (2001). Parenting stress in families of children with disabilities. *American Journal of Orthopsychiatry, 71*, 257-261.

Wechsler, D. (2002). *Wechsler Preschool and Primary Scale of Intelligence: Third Edition, Administration and Scoring Manual*. San Antonio, TX: The Psychological Corporation.

Weiner, H. M. (2003). Effective inclusion: Professional development in the context of the classroom. *Teaching Exceptional Children, 35*(6), 12-18.

Zaccario, M., Salsberg, D., Gordon, R., & Bilginer, L. (2009). Psychological and neuropsychological issues in the care of children with disabilities. *Journal of Pediatric Rehabilitation Medicine, 2*, 93-99.

www.ingramcontent.com/pod-product-compliance
Lightning Source LLC
Chambersburg PA
CBHW071133280326
41935CB00010B/1211